THE BRITISH BIBLIOGRAPHY OF EDGAR WALLACE

THE
BRITISH
BIBLIOGRAPHY
OF
EDGAR WALLACE

W.O.G. Lofts and Derek Adley

HOWARD BAKER
London

W.O.G. Lofts and Derek Adley
THE BRITISH BIBLIOGRAPHY OF
EDGAR WALLACE

First published by Howard Baker Publishers
Limited, 1969

A HOWARD BAKER BOOK

SBN O9 304760 6

Howard Baker books are published by
HOWARD BAKER PUBLISHERS LIMITED
47 Museum Street, London, W.C.1

Printed and bound in Great Britain by
Balding & Mansell Ltd, of London and Wisbech

Contents

The British Bibliography of Edgar Wallace

Leslie Charteris writes . . .

Shakespeare and Dickens were never thought of as 'classics' in their own day. They were just 'popular writers'.

So was Edgar Wallace. But I have long had a feeling that his chance of being the 'classis' of some future century is as good as theirs. He not only surpassed them in this legendary output, but in his extraordinary versatility, which I don't think any other writer ever equalled. And if a great deal of literary merit attaches to brilliant depiction of a period or inspired prophecy of one to come, surely Wallace's 'fantastic' crime stories (which were far from his only product) cannot be scoffed at today as any more ridiculous than the scientific fantasies of Jules Verne.

I hope that this bibliography will help future critics as well as old *aficionados* like myself to appreciate his real greatness.

W. O. G. Lofts is, in my opinion, a researcher of really phenomenal ability, ingenuity and thoroughness. I had the pleasure of publishing the results of several of his enquiries in the form of articles in the *Saint Magazine*. Besides that, he has devoted his unusual talent to a number of other research projects which I personally asked him to undertake, always with the most interesting results. I cannot speak too highly of the flair and perseverance which he brings to the digging up of deeply buried facts.

Introduction
by Penelope Wallace

Some eight years ago I compiled a list of my father's books with alternate titles as far as I could trace them. I intended to follow it up with a list of short stories and I even thought of compiling a bibliography but the immense importance of such a work was balanced by the immense amount of research and care which I knew it would need. When I heard that W. O. G. Lofts and D. J. Adley were compiling a bibliography, my hopes rose and when I saw the completed manuscript, they were fulfilled because here, without any effort on my part, was the most complete record of one of, if not the most, prolific writers the world has ever known.

This is the record of a man who, apart from plays and film scripts, covered every format in which the printed word is published; whose professionalism enabled him to write specifically to any required length by any stated time and yet whose enthusiasm fills every page and gives lasting life to his characters.

When an author is alive it is fairly simple to compile a bibliography because he can be expected to recall approximately what he wrote and usually when an author is dead there will be records; and books can be traced through his publishers.

My father's books have been issued in England by at least thirty publishers. They were serialised under one title, published in England under another and frequently, in America, under a further one and the problem of reconciling these is great, particularly as the opening lines are not necessarily the same.

Edgar Wallace was not greatly concerned with such things as records and office routine—an example occurred when he planned to bring back from Germany a competant English-speaking assistant secretary who had been well-recommended to him. Instead the girl asked him to take her younger sister for political reasons. This he did and when his secretary asked what help the new assistant could be as she could neither read nor write a word of English, he said, 'She can do the filing.'

After his death, lists were compiled from various sources but they are cautiously marked, 'as far as can be traced.' My mother could have dealt with the matter but other problems claimed her time which was limited. She died in the following year and it is a constant surprise to me that for almost thirty years, no-one including his biographer, made any attempt to verify the number of books my father wrote.

His immense output has given his work a legendary quality though it is not sentiment which makes people read his books today, it is the fact that his stories have fast moving plots and are written in a simple style, and it is interesting to note that, until recently, this compact writing was more readily found in America than in Britain.

Apart from the quality of readability he has the more elusive one of re-readability. A thriller has peaks of action and between the peaks are the valleys where the reader can be lost—overnight or forever; in these valleys it is imperative that reader interest should be sustained. Edgar Wallace does this by the soundness of his minor characterisation and by his humour and it is these valleys which enable one to re-read even when the peaks are known in advance.

His minor characters were sound because he loved and understood people. I realise that it is no coincidence that humour and humanity have the same root but people are often unaware how closely they are allied. Both imply the ability to see what is basically true, but require self-honesty. Pomposity and humour do not go together nor can the Pharisee judge his fellows.

A further reason for my father's continued success is his lack of bitterness. There are occasions when he is angry particularly on such subjects as 'baby farming' but none when hatred—specific or general—obscures the test. His villains are usually English and on the rare occasions when they are not home-grown they are imported impartially. The villain of *The Yellow Snake* is Chinese as is the hero of *The Clue of The New Pin*. There is no trace of racial or religious prejudice and it is rare for the villain to be completely bad. Those who say that his characters are either black or white can never have read his books. Few of his bad men are disallowed a redeeming feature or a moment of goodness.

People often ask me what it was like to be my father's daughter. Firstly he was fond of children. He treated me as an equal—discussing any query without a hint of patronage. He was entirely approachable, the study door was never locked and I was never told to keep away. Such were his powers of concentration that he could stop dictating, switch his mind to my problems and, when I left, switch straight back to whatever he had been writing.

I inherited much of his character and I acquired from him much of his philosophy of life, a philosophy of optimism for the future and no regrets for the past. He had, too, an extreme intolerance of affection and falseness and of self-pity.

But consciously I believe that being Edgar Wallace's daughter has meant more to me since I was adult than when he was alive. It has meant an enormous friendliness—not just from people who knew my father in person but from all those who have read his books. They have affection for him both for the pleasure he has given and for himself as they know him from his books. My father's complete self-honesty makes it apparent to the reader that he is not a man who writes one thing and believes or lives another.

Often publishers pass on to me formal queries or enquiries about my father's books and when I reply direct I receive in return a letter as to the daughter of a friend. It is this warmth which I believe most clearly shows the quality of my father's work and gives me the same pleasure that I know it would give him.

Foreword

When Derek Adley suggested to me some years ago that we compile a bibliography of the works of Edgar Wallace published in the United Kingdom, I readily agreed. To be honest, I thought that the task would not be too difficult, and everyone to whom I spoke at the time was in agreement that such a project would be very worthwhile.

Since then, Derek and I have spent hundreds of hours in research, poring over thousands of books, newspapers and magazines, and today no-one could know better than we do what a phenomenon—in every sense of that word—Edgar Wallace was.

There is no doubt at all in our minds that he was, without question, the most prolific writer of popular fiction that the world has ever known. Even now we are far from being certain that we have traced all of the stories he published in Britain—though we are confident that we have tracked down and recorded all of his books—and is it only because of the growing impatience of so many of his admirers to see the results of our labours in print that Derek and I have decided to publish the results of our researches to date.

At the outset, as I have said, I thought it would be a fairly simple task to trace all the works of Edgar Wallace which have been published in the United Kingdom. I could not have been more wrong. It has proved to be a most laborious business. For Wallace's output was truly prodigious, and he himself kept few records, and of the few that he did keep none is anywhere close to being complete. Furthermore, that favoured recourse of the British bibliographer, the British Museum, has been unable to assist authoritatively in this instance either, since many of its files of the popular magazines of the Twenties, which contained the bulk of first publications of Wallace's work, were destroyed in the Blitz.

That same rain of fire burned great gaps in publishers' libraries of file copies, too, and though private collectors have given their unstinted assistance both to Derek and to myself—here acknowledged with our gratitude—many issues of *Grand Magazine* and *Yes or No* (both particularly rich sources of Edgar Wallace material) remain untraced, and perhaps untraceable.

Nevertheless, it is our proud claim that this is not only the first bibliography of Edgar Wallace's British publications to be issued, but that it is also the most detailed that anyone after a mere four years of labour could possibly compile. Not only does it list books by Edgar Wallace which have so far gone unrecorded by the British Museum —such as *Killer Kay* and *The Lady Called Nita*—but it also includes information regarding dozens of stories, and even some serials, which for one reason or another Edgar Wallace never brought together into book form. These are probably now brought to the notice of many readers here for the very first time.

Throughout, it is true to say, most of the major difficulties which Derek and I have encountered have concerned magazines to which Wallace contributed, many of which—even with my specialist's knowledge of this field— were completely unknown to me, and the vast majority of which have long since passed into oblivion.

Unfailing sources of irritation along the way have been the erroneous, and often downright misleading, brief bibliographies contained in all too many of the multitudinous books about Edgar Wallace. A little more care on the part of their authors would have saved Derek Adley and I many hours of fruitless research. Even the normally most accurate and efficient late Robert Curtis, who did such noble work for Edgar Wallace as his secretary, cannot be adjudged guiltless in this respect. He slipped up badly when he stated that Wallace wrote only one serial under the pseudonym of Richard Cloud. Not only did Wallace write three serials under this name in *Answers*, but Curtis got the title of the one he did list quite wrong.

Probably the one thing that caused greatest annoyance to Edgar Wallace during his lifetime was the persistent rumour that, in view of his tremendous output, he must have employed ghost writers to help him. Certainly, in the course of my researches, I have found no evidence whatsoever to support this contention. Indeed, on the contrary, I have found that Wallace himself 'ghosted' for quite a few people—particularly where articles were concerned.

Which brings me to the last point that I have to make.

Whilst this is primarily a story bibliography, we have included many articles written by Edgar Wallace where they are of more than an ephemeral interest: ephemeral in this instance meaning principally concerned with horse-racing in the 'twenties and early 'thirties, an interest which held Wallace in its grip, and cost him vast sums of money, right up to the end of his life.

Finally, Derek Adley and I can only hope that this bibliography will give as much pleasure and interest to its readers as it has given to us in its compilation. We are aware of, and apologise for, its many deficiencies. Please help us—with information—to make the next edition more complete and all-embracing than this one.

W. O. G. Lofts

London, April 1969

EDGAR WALLACE BOOKS
BY YEAR OF PUBLICATION

Year	*Ref.*	*Title*	*Publisher*
1898	B108	THE MISSION THAT FAILED.	T. Maskew Miller (South Africa)
1900	B165	WAR AND OTHER POEMS.	Eastern Press (South Africa)
	B171	WRIT IN BARRACKS.	Methuen
1901	B163	UNOFFICIAL DISPATCHES.	Hutchinson
1905	B61	THE FOUR JUST MEN.	Tallis Press
	B140	SMITHY.	Tallis Press
1908	B6	ANGEL ESQUIRE.	Arrowsmith/ Simpkin Marshall
	B33	THE COUNCIL OF JUSTICE.	Ward Lock
1909	B25	CAPTAIN TATHAM OF TATHAM ISLAND.	Gale & Polden
	B141	SMITHY ABROAD.	Hulton
	B45	THE DUKE IN THE SUBURBS.	Ward Lock
1910	B116	THE NINE BEARS.	Ward Lock
1911	B135	SANDERS OF THE RIVER.	Ward Lock
1912	B125	THE PEOPLE OF THE RIVER.	Ward Lock
	B128	PRIVATE SELBY	Ward Lock
1913	B63	THE FOURTH PLAGUE.	Ward Lock
	B74	GREY TIMOTHY.	Ward Lock
	B131	THE RIVER OF STARS.	Ward Lock
1914	B1	THE ADMIRABLE CARFEW.	Ward Lock
	B21	BOSAMBO OF THE RIVER.	Ward Lock
	B49	FAMOUS SCOTTISH REGIMENTS.	Newnes
	B52	FIELD MARSHAL SIR JOHN FRENCH.	Newnes
	B79	HEROES ALL : GALLANT DEEDS OF THE WAR	Newnes

Year	Ref.	Title	Publisher
	B146	STANDARD HISTORY OF THE WAR.	Newnes
1915	**B16**	BONES.	Ward Lock
	B89	KITCHENER'S ARMY AND THE TERRITORIAL FORCES.	Newnes
	B100	THE MAN WHO BOUGHT LONDON.	Ward Lock
	B104	THE MELODY OF DEATH.	Arrowsmith/ Simpkin Marshall
	B117	'1925' THE STORY OF A FATAL PEACE.	Newnes
	B142	SMITHY AND THE HUN.	Newnes
	B166	VOL. 2–4. WAR OF THE NATIONS.	Newnes
1916	**B39**	A DEBT DISCHARGED.	Ward Lock
	B118	NOBBY.	Newnes
	B159	THE TOMB OF T'SIN.	Ward Lock
	B166	VOL. 5–7. WAR OF THE NATIONS.	Newnes
1917	**B84**	THE JUST MEN OF CORDOVA.	Ward Lock
	B86	THE KEEPERS OF THE KINGS PEACE.	Newnes
	B137	THE SECRET HOUSE.	Newnes
	B166	VOL. 8–9. WAR OF THE NATIONS.	Newnes
1918	**B31**	THE CLUE OF THE TWISTED CANDLE.	Newnes
	B44	DOWN UNDER DONOVAN.	Ward Lock
	B95	LIEUTENANT BONES.	Ward Lock
	B150	TAM OF THE SCOUTS.	Newnes
	B156	THOSE FOLK OF BULBORO.	Ward Lock
1919	**B2**	THE ADVENTURES OF HEINE.	Ward Lock

Books by Year of Publication

Year	Ref.	Title	Publisher
	B53	THE FIGHTING SCOUTS.	Pearson
	B73	THE GREEN RUST.	Ward Lock
	B85	KATE PLUS TEN.	Ward Lock
	B102	THE MAN WHO KNEW.	Newnes
1920	**B35**	THE DAFFODIL MYSTERY.	Ward Lock
	B82	JACK O'JUDGMENT.	Ward Lock
1921	**B17**	BONES IN LONDON.	Ward Lock
	B19	THE BOOK OF ALL POWER.	Ward Lock
	B94	THE LAW OF THE FOUR JUST MEN.	Hodder & Stoughton
1922	**B7**	THE ANGEL OF TERROR.	Hodder & Stoughton
	B34	THE CRIMSON CIRCLE.	Hodder & Stoughton
	B56	THE FLYING FIFTY-FIVE.	Hutchinson
	B111	MR. JUSTICE MAXELL.	Ward Lock
	B136	SANDI THE KING MAKER.	Ward Lock
	B164	THE VALLEY OF GHOSTS.	Odhams
1923	**B18**	BONES OF THE RIVER.	Newnes
	B20	THE BOOKS OF BART.	Ward Lock
	B24	CAPTAINS OF SOULS.	John Long
	B27	CHICK.	Ward Lock
	B29	THE CLUE OF THE NEW PIN.	Hodder & Stoughton
	B70	THE GREEN ARCHER.	Hodder & Stoughton
	B107	THE MISSING MILLION.	John Long
1924	**B36**	THE DARK EYES OF LONDON.	Ward Lock
	B43	DOUBLE DAN.	Hodder & Stoughton
	B46	EDUCATED EVANS.	Webster
	B48	THE FACE IN THE NIGHT.	John Long

Year	*Ref.*	*Title*	*Publisher*
	B132	ROOM 13.	John Long
	B139	THE SINISTER MAN.	Hodder & Stoughton
	B158	THE THREE OAK MYSTERY.	Ward Lock
1925	**B14**	THE BLACK AVONS.	G. Gill
	B15	THE BLUE HAND.	Ward Lock
	B37	THE DAUGHTERS OF THE NIGHT.	Newnes
	B51	THE FELLOWSHIP OF THE FROG.	Ward Lock
	B65	THE GAUNT STRANGER.	Hodder & Stoughton
	B88	A KING BY NIGHT.	John Long
	B106	THE MIND OF MR. J. G. REEDER.	Hodder & Stoughton
	B148	THE STRANGE COUNTESS.	Hodder & Stoughton
1926	**B8**	THE AVENGER.	John Long
	B9	BARBARA ON HER OWN.	Newnes
	B13	THE BLACK ABBOT.	Hodder & Stoughton
	B38	THE DAY OF UNITING.	Hodder & Stoughton
	B41	THE DOOR WITH SEVEN LOCKS.	Hodder & Stoughton
	B83	THE JOKER.	Hodder & Stoughton
	B99	THE MAN FROM MOROCCO.	John Long
	B105	THE MILLION DOLLAR STORY.	Newnes
	B113	MORE EDUCATED EVANS.	Webster
	B119	THE NORTHING TRAMP.	Hodder & Stoughton

Books by Year of Publication

Year	Ref.	Title	Publisher
	B123	'PENELOPE' OF THE POLYANTHA.	Hodder & Stoughton
	B124	PEOPLE.	Hodder & Stoughton
	B134	SANDERS.	Hodder & Stoughton
	B144	THE SQUARE EMERALD.	Hodder & Stoughton
	B151	THE TERRIBLE PEOPLE.	Hodder & Stoughton
	B157	THE THREE JUST MEN.	Hodder & Stoughton
	B167	WE SHALL SEE.	Hodder & Stoughton
	B172	THE YELLOW SNAKE.	Hodder & Stoughton
1927	**B10**	BIG FOOT.	John Long
	B22	THE BRIGAND.	Hodder & Stoughton
	B50	THE FEATHERED SERPENT	Hodder & Stoughton
	B55	FLAT 2.	John Long
	B58	THE FORGER	Hodder & Stoughton
	B68	GOOD EVANS.	Webster
	B78	THE HAND OF POWER.	John Long
	B103	THE MAN WHO WAS NOBODY.	Ward Lock
	B112	THE MIXER.	John Long
	B120	NUMBER SIX.	Newnes
	B145	THE SQUEAKER.	Hodder & Stoughton

Year	Ref.	Title	Publisher
	B153	TERROR KEEP.	Hodder & Stoughton
	B155	THIS ENGLAND.	Hodder & Stoughton
	B160	THE TRAITOR'S GATE.	Hodder & Stoughton
1928	**B3**	AGAIN SAUNDERS.	Hodder & Stoughton
	B42	THE DOUBLE.	Hodder & Stoughton
	B47	ELEGANT EDWARD.	Readers Library
	B57	THE FLYING SQUAD.	Hodder & Stoughton
	B75	THE GUNNER.	John Long
	B122	THE ORATOR.	Hutchinson
	B154	THE THIEF IN THE NIGHT.	Readers Library
	B161	THE TWISTER.	John Long
1929	**B4**	AGAIN THE RINGER.	Hodder & Stoughton
	B5	AGAIN THE THREE JUST MEN.	Hodder & Stoughton
	B11	THE BIG FOUR.	Readers Library
	B12	THE BLACK.	Readers Library
	B26	THE CAT BURGLAR.	Newnes
	B28	CIRCUMSTANTIAL EVIDENCE.	Newnes
	B54	FIGHTING SNUB REILLY.	Newnes
	B59	FOR INFORMATION RECEIVED.	Newnes
	B60	FORTY-EIGHT SHORT STORIES.	Newnes
	B62	FOUR SQUARE JANE.	Readers Library
	B66	THE GHOST OF DOWNHILL.	Readers Library
	B67	THE GOLDEN HADES.	Collins

6

Books by Year of Publication

Year	Ref.	Title	Publisher
	B69	THE GOVERNOR OF CHI-FOO.	Newnes
	B72	THE GREEN RIBBON.	Hutchinson
	B80	THE INDIA RUBBER MEN.	Hodder & Stoughton
	B92	THE LADY OF LITTLE HELL.	Newnes
	B96	THE LITTLE GREEN MAN.	Newnes
	B97	THE LONE HOUSE MYSTERY.	Collins
	B126	PLANETOID 127.	Readers Library
	B127	THE PRISON BREAKERS.	Newnes
	B129	RED ACES.	Hodder & Stoughton
	B130	THE REPORTER.	Readers Library
	B152	THE TERROR.	Collins
1930	**B23**	THE CALENDAR.	Collins
	B30	THE CLUE OF THE SILVER KEY.	Hodder & Stoughton
	B81	THE IRON GRIP.	Readers Library
	B87	KILLER KAY.	Newnes
	B90	THE LADY CALLED NITA.	Newnes
	B91	THE LADY OF ASCOT.	Hutchinson
	B109	MRS. WILLIAM JONES & BILL.	Newnes
	B169	WHITE FACE.	Hodder & Stoughton
1931	**B32**	THE COAT OF ARMS.	Hutchinson
	B40	THE DEVIL MAN.	Collins
	B98	THE MAN AT THE CARLTON.	Hodder & Stoughton
	B121	ON THE SPOT.	John Long
1932	**B64**	THE FRIGHTENED LADY.	Hodder & Stoughton
	B76	THE GUV'NOR & OTHER STORIES.	Collins

7

Year	Ref.	Title	Publisher
	B77	THE GUV'NOR.	Collins
	B115	MY HOLLYWOOD DIARY.	Hutchinson
	B138	SERGEANT SIR PETER.	Chapman & Hall
	B147	THE STEWARD.	Collins
	B168	WHEN THE GANGS CAME TO LONDON.	John Long
1933	**B71***	THE GREEN PACK (R. CURTIS).	Hutchinson
1934	**B93**	THE LAST ADVENTURE.	Hutchinson
	B110	MR. J. G. REEDER RETURNS.	Collins
	B170	THE WOMAN FROM THE EAST.	Hutchinson
1935	**B101***	THE MAN WHO CHANGED HIS NAME (R. CURTIS).	Hutchinson
	B114*	THE MOUTHPIECE (E. W. & R. CURTIS).	Hutchinson
1936	**B133***	SANCTUARY ISLAND (R. CURTIS).	Hutchinson
	B143*	SMOKY CELL (R. CURTIS).	Hutchinson
	B149	THE TABLE (R. CURTIS).	Hutchinson
1963	**B162**	THE UNDISCLOSED CLIENT	Digit Books

*Notes.**

Novelisation of Edgar Wallace plays and films by Robert Curtis. B114 was written jointly by them.

1. An earlier edition of B118 'Nobby' has since been discovered dated 1914, and published by Town Topics Office, entitled 'Smithys Friend Nobby'.

2. B166. 'War of the Nations' is now known to have had two further Vols. 10–11. It is not possible to give any details about this work, as no record can be found of it in Library files.

8

SHORT STORIES

The following series of short stories or single short stories are listed as having been written probably for magazine publication. They did not appear in book form—nor have they been traced in magazines. They are printed by kind permission of Edgar Wallace Ltd.

Series of Short Stories

ADVENTURES OF AIRMAN HAY. (9 stories)
COMPANIONS OF THE ACE HIGH. (6 stories)
EARL OF NOWHERE. (4 stories)
END OF THE KAISER. (15 stories)
SECRETS OF ESCAPES FROM PRISON CAMPS. (4 stories)
JOCKS AT THE FRONT. (6 stories)
MURDER SERIES. (6 stories)
MY MURDERERS. (5 stories)
PRIVATE NANCY. (21 stories)
TALES OF THE TANKS. (4 stories)
THOSE GERMANS. (10 stories)
SCOT ON THE ATTACK, THE (5 stories)

Short Stories

ARISTOCRATIC TAXI-DRIVER.
BANK OF ENGLAND FRAUDS, THE
BIG IF.
BLUE BICYCLE CASE, THE
BRIDGES OF THE RHINE.
DARE-DEVIL TOMMY IN GERMANY.
EMPEROR OF THE BRITISH.
ERSATZ KAISER.
EVELYN.
GEORGE'S FRIENDS.
GOGS JOINS HIS UNIT.
HOW MANIE CAME TO LONDON.

IF I WERE THE KAISER.
LEAGUE OF YOUTH, THE
LONELY OFFICER, THE
MAN, THE WIFE, THE GIRL, THE
MAGNIFICENT ENSIGN SMITH, THE
MAKINGS UP OF HERBERT STAGG.
MARKSMEN OF ENGLAND.
MEN OF ALLIED ARMIES.
MYSTERIOUS WAY.
ONE NIGHT IN SOMERSET.
PICCADILLY SLEUTH, THE
PRIVATE OF THE LINE.
REVELATIONS OF DR. GALLOWS, THE
SPY OF THE THREE NATIONS, THE
STRANGE CASE OF LARRY SIEGLEMANN, THE
SUFFRAGIST'S HUSBAND.
TALE-TELLER.
TREMENDOUS JONES, THE
UNDER FIRE.
WHITE CHRISTMAS.

RARE EDITIONS

It is obvious to assume that books and novels only published once are the rarest, and this certainly has proved the case by collectors of Wallaciana in Great Britain. The scarcest items are his first, just before the turn of the century—a slim volume of verses entitled 'The Mission that Failed' and published out in South Africa at a shilling. In his autobiography entitled 'People' on 1926, Edgar Wallace stated 'that he had not got a copy, and would gladly give a "tenner" (£10) for one.' His second publication, likewise a pamphlet of verses price three-pence, and published in the same country, must run it very close. I have yet to hear of anyone having a copy of either outside the British Museum.

'Smithy Abroad' is also very rare, when the only copy known to exist is in a Library at Oxford. England, whilst the Newnes paperback 'Killer Kay' must come next, as Derek J. Adley, has the only copy known in existence in his collection. Likewise, a copy of 'The Lady called Nita' which was similar in format, though another copy of this was known to be in circulation some years ago. Many of the Newnes publications were in paperback form, and because they were in that format they have not survived through the years like bound books, and so consequently are rarer than many others.

In the field of actual bound books, there is no doubt that 'The Tomb of T'Sin' (Ward Lock 1916) is the rarest. A secondhand bookseller, who is also an Edgar Wallace enthusiast, has yet to see a copy in the hundreds of thousands of books passing through his hands in the last twenty-five years. Having had the pleasure of reading this blue-covered book with gold lettering in the British Museum, I can vouch for the fact, that it is a first class story with a Chinese and mystery background, which was Wallace at his best.

With no trace of it ever being reprinted, or record of it

being serialised in a magazine, like many of his full length novels. It is rather extraordinary, as this tale could be classed as a classic.

The historical four volumes of the 'Black Avons' are also very rare, with one collector known to have the full set, and odd volumes turning up from time to time. Of magazine stories, 'Yes, or No' seem the rarest, and if only volumes could be located in the 1908–15 period, they would probably produce some interesting 'new' material. An odd copy in the hands of a collector, shows a story so far not traced elsewhere.

'Hush' is another magazine, now seemingly lost in the mists of time, of which Edgar Wallace was the editor in 1930, and which contained some of his stories. Whilst finally it is presumed that Wallace probably wrote far more for the Thomson magazine group, than that has been discovered. He thought so much of this firm that he dedicated 'The Strange Countess' (1925) 'with the author's happiest memories of a long business association.'

FIRST EDITIONS

One of the most difficult tasks in compiling this bibliography, was establishing, and recording, the exact first edition of an Edgar Wallace book. As already mentioned in the foreward, unfortunately the British Museum does not have a complete record of all his works. Also, some of the books found there, and recorded are not strictly the first editions. One cannot blame them for this, as through the years, it is possible that some were either mislaid, or destroyed by fire during the last war.

Such was the popularity of Edgar Wallace, that his books sold in millions, consequently dozens and dozens of reprints were made, and it would take a whole library in itself to store all his editions and impressions made of his books, and certainly only a fraction of these are recorded in Museum files. Publishers did not help matters at all, by not dating their first editions, and with later editions likewise not dated and similar in appearance, it is almost an impossibility in some cases to define them, because of this practice.

If publishers had stuck to a certain rule, one could have easily stated that a certain firm either dated or undated books, but this was not so. Hodder and Stoughton for instance did not date their first editions, but did so in the later ones, sometimes with roman numerals. Ward Lock did the exact opposite, and dated their first issues, and not the later ones.

Newnes, went in between, and dated some and not the majority of others. John Long dated theirs, but even so, readers must be wary of at least 'The Face in the Night' which came out in the Spring of 1924, proved by an advert in its pages advising readers that other books would be ready by Winter 1924, yet it has a 1925 publishers copyright mark.

One could at least establish if the British Museum copy

was a 'first' or not, by the official Museum month and year stamp inside the cover. That is a record of when the book was received by them from the publishers as required by law. Publishers themselves can give no explanation for their strange policies in not defining first editions, some give the extraordinary statement that this is left to the whims of the printers!

In many cases, no explanation is needed in defining a first edition, and that is where a book or novel was only published once, or where the original publisher likewise had only one issue on the market. Both these cases are of course clearly indicated in the bibliography.

Whilst this is only a British bibliography, it is also interesting to point out that at least one book was published in the U.S.A. some two years before it was published in Great Britain. This was 'Kate Plus Ten' (Small Maynard & Co. of Boston) in 1917, so correctly speaking the American edition is actually the very first.

As it is appreciated that many Librarians, Collectors, and Book Dealers, are anxious to recognise the first edition of any book, we have indicated and given the most details possible, but we do ask them to bear with us in the extreme difficulties encountered in this problem. We can do nothing better, than to invite readers to write to us on any difficulty on the subject, and will be pleased to conduct further research on any problems.

CLASSIFICATION OF FIRST EDITIONS

B1   THE ADMIRABLE CARFEW.   Ward Lock
Cr. 8vo. Designed cover.   1914
Illustrated. Dated 1914. Pages
11–315; 1, 2, 3, & 7. Dedicated
to : My Friend, C.E.L.

B2   THE ADVENTURES OF HEINE.   Ward Lock
Cr. 8vo. Illustrated. Dated 1919.   1919
Pages 9–319.

B3   AGAIN SANDERS.   Hodder &
Cr. 8vo. Undated. Pages 7–315.   Stoughton
To : Lord Dewar.   1928

B4   AGAIN THE RINGER.   Hodder &
Cr. 8vo. Undated. Pages 9–315;   Stoughton
1–4. Dedicated to : My Genial   1929.
and Brilliant Friend Walter
Hackett.

B5   AGAIN THE THREE JUST MEN.   Hodder &
Cr. 8vo. Undated. Pages 8–320.   Stoughton
To : George Dilnot.   1929.

B6   ANGEL ESQUIRE.   J. Arrowsmith/
Cr. 8vo. Illustrated Cover.   Simpkin Marshall
Undated. 299 pages.   1908
Dedicated to : F.T.S.

B7   THE ANGEL OF TERROR.   Hodder &
Cr. 8vo. Undated. Pages 5–320.   Stoughton
To : F.L.S., A Man of Law.   1922

B8   THE AVENGER   John Long
Cr. 8vo. Dated Reverse to title   1926
page 1926. Pages 5–318; 1–31.

B9   BARBARA ON HER OWN.   Newnes
Cr. 8vo. Undated. Pages 11–190.   1926

B10   BIG FOOT.   John Long
Cr. 8vo. Dated reverse to title   1927
page: 1927. Pages 9–286.

B11   THE BIG FOUR.   Readers Library
Fcp. 8vo. Undated. Pages 10   1929
and 14–188.

B12   THE BLACK.   Readers Library
Fcp. 8vo. Undated. Pages   1929
10–189.

B13   THE BLACK ABBOT   Hodder &
Cr. 8vo. Undated. Pages 5–319.   Stoughton
To: The Rev. A. V. C. Hordern   1926
of Market Drayton, a friend of
soldiers.

B14   THE BLACK AVONS   G. Gill
Cr. 8vo. All four Vols. have   1925
illustrated covers. All dated
1925.
1. How they fared in the Times
   of the Tudors. Pages 2–81.
2. Roundhead and Cavalier.
   Pages 2–72.
3. From Waterloo to the
   Mutiny. Pages 2–70.
4. Europe in the Melting Pot.
   Pages 2–75.

B15   THE BLUE HAND.   Ward Lock
Cr. 8vo. Dated 1925.   1925
Pages 5–288.

B16   BONES.   Ward Lock
Cr. 8vo. Dated 1915.   1915
Illustrated Cover. Illustrated.
Pages 9–304; 1–16. To: Isabel
Thorn who was largely
responsible for bringing

Sanders into being this book is
dedicated.

B17   BONES IN LONDON.   Ward Lock
Cr. 8vo. Illustrated. Dated   1921
1921. Pages 5; 7–316.

B18   BONES OF THE RIVER.   Newnes
Cr. 8vo. Undated. Pages 9–249. 1923

B19   THE BOOK OF ALL POWER.   Ward Lock
Cr. 8vo. Dated 1921. Pages 1–4; 1921
11–13; 15–301. To: Harry
Hughes-Onslow.

B20   THE BOOKS OF BART.   Ward Lock
Cr. 8vo. Undated. Pages 5;   1923
9–304; 2–16.

B21   BOSAMBO OF THE RIVER.   Ward Lock
Cr. 8vo. Illustrated cover.   1914
Illustrated. Dated 1914.
Pages 7–304; 1–16.

B22   THE BRIGAND.   Hodder &
Cr. 8vo. Part illustrated cover. Stoughton
Undated. Pages 5; 7–312,   1927

B23   THE CALENDAR.   Collins
Cr. 8vo. Dated reverse to title 1930
page. 1930. Pages 7–288.
Dedicated to the great sportsman
H.H. The Prince Aga Khan.

B24   CAPTAINS OF SOULS.   John Long
Cr. 8vo. Designed spine.   1923
Dated reverse to title page
1923. Pages 7–318; 2–15.

B25   CAPTAIN TATHAM OF TATHAM Gale & Polden
       ISLAND.   1909
Stiff paperback. 7″ × 5″.

Illustrated cover. Dated 1909.
133 pages.

B26   THE CAT BURGLAR.   Newnes
       Paperback. 8″ × 5″ illustrated   1929
       cover. Undated. Pages 5–127.

B27   CHICK.   Ward Lock
       Cr. 8vo. Dated 1923 reverse to   1923
       title page. Pages 5; 7–311; 1–8.

B28   CIRCUMSTANTIAL EVIDENCE.   Newnes
       8″ × 5½″ Paperback. Illustrated   1929
       cover. Undated. Pages 5–128.

B29   THE CLUE OF THE NEW PIN.   Hodder &
       Cr. 8vo. Undated. Pages 5–319.   Stoughton
       Dedicated to: C. Grenville Page.   1923

B30   THE CLUE OF THE SILVER KEY.   Hodder &
       Cr. 8vo. Undated. Pages 5–317.   Stoughton
       Dedicated to Michael Beary.   1930

B31   THE CLUE OF THE TWISTED   Newnes
       CANDLE.   1918
       Small Cr. 8vo. Designed cover.
       Undated. Pages 5–254.

B32   THE COAT OF ARMS.   Hutchinson
       Cr. 8vo. Undated. Pages 9–288.   1931
       Three-Thirty-two (written)
       To: My Friend Karen Ostrer.

B33   THE COUNCIL OF JUSTICE   Ward Lock
       Cr. 8vo. Illustrated by Alec Ball.   1908
       Dated 1908. Pages 7–319; 1–16.
       Dedicated to I. M. W.

B34   THE CRIMSON CIRCLE.   Hodder &
       Cr. 8vo. Undated. Pages   Stoughton
       v, vi, vii, viii; 9–320.   1922
       To: Brian.

B35 THE DAFFODIL MYSTERY.   Ward Lock
Cr. 8vo. Dated 1920. Pages   1920
6–307.

B36 THE DARK EYES OF LONDON.   Ward Lock
Cr. 8vo. 312 pages. No other   1924
details known.

B37 THE DAUGHTERS OF THE NIGHT.   Newnes
Stiff Paperback. 7″ × 5″.   1925
Illustrated cover. Undated.
Pages 5–127.

B38 THE DAY OF UNITING.   Hodder &
7″ × 4½″ Designed cover.   Stoughton
Undated. Pages 5–314.   1926

B39 A DEBT DISCHARGED.   Ward Lock
Cr. 8vo. Designed cover.   1916
Illustrated. Dated 1916.
Pages 8–303; 1–16.

B40 THE DEVIL MAN.   Collins
Cr. 8vo. Dated 1931 reverse to   1931
title page. Pages 5–317.

B41 THE DOOR WITH SEVEN LOCKS.   Hodder &
Cr. 8vo. Part illustrated cover.   Stoughton
Undated. Pages 5–319.   1926
Dedication: To My Friend
H. B. Lawford Esq. (A just man)
Worshipful Master of the
Drapers Company. 1925–1926.

B42 THE DOUBLE.   Hodder &
Cr. 8vo. Undated.   Stoughton
Pages 5–320.   1928

B43 DOUBLE DAN.   Hodder &
Cr. 8vo. Undated.   Stoughton
Pages 5–320.   1924

B44 DOWN UNDER DONOVAN. Ward Lock
Cr. 8vo. Designed cover. 1918
Undated. Pages 5–254.

B45 THE DUKE IN THE SUBURBS. Ward Lock
Cr. 8vo. Illustrated. Dated 1909. 1909
Pages 7–304; 1–16.
Dedication to: Marion
Caldecott with the author's
humble Homage.

B46 EDUCATED EVANS. Webster
Cr. 8vo. Undated. 1924
Pages 5; 7–285

B47 ELEGANT EDWARD. Readers Library
Fcp. 8vo. Undated. 1928
Pages 9–182.

B48 THE FACE IN THE NIGHT. John Long
Cr. 8vo. Dated 1925 reverse to 1924
title page and on page 318.
Pages v, vi; 7–318; 1–29.

B49 FAMOUS SCOTTISH REGIMENTS. Newnes
Large paperback. $11'' \times 8\frac{1}{2}''$. 1914
Illustrated cover. Illustrated.
Undated. Pages 2–30.

B50 THE FEATHERED SERPENT. Hodder &
Cr. 8vo. Undated. Pages 5–312. Stoughton
To: Daphne Du Maurier. 1927

B51 THE FELLOWSHIP OF THE FROG. Ward Lock
Cr. 8vo. Dated 1925. 1925
Pages 5–288

B52 FIELD MARSHAL SIR JOHN Newnes
FRENCH. 1914
Large paperback. $11'' \times 8\frac{1}{2}''$.
Illustrated cover. Illustrated.
Undated. Pages 2–30.

B53 THE FIGHTING SCOUTS. Pearson
7″ × 4½″ designed cover. Dated 1919
1919. Pages 116.

B54 FIGHTING SNUB O'REILLY. Newnes
8″ × 5½″ paperback. Illustrated 1929
cover. Undated. Pages 5–127.

B55 FLAT 2. John Long
Cr. 8vo. Dated 1927 reverse to 1927
title page. Pages v, vi; 7–286.

B56 THE FLYING FIFTY-FIVE. Hutchinson
Cr. 8vo. Undated. Pages ix, x; 1922
11–287. To: My Colleagues and
Friends of the Sporting Press
this book is affectionately
dedicated.

B57 THE FLYING SQUAD. Hodder &
Cr. 8vo. Undated. Pages 7–312. Stoughton
To: My Young Friend Lady 1928
Pamela Smith.

B58 THE FORGER. Hodder &
Cr. 8vo. Undated. Pages 5–312. Stoughton
To: Dennis Neilson Terry. 1927

B59 FOR INFORMATION RECEIVED. Newnes
Paperback. 8″ × 5½″. 1929
Illustrated cover. Pages 5–127.
Undated.

B60 FORTY-EIGHT SHORT STORIES. Newnes
Cr. 8vo. Undated. Pages vii, 1929
viii; 1–1014.

B61 THE FOUR JUST MEN. Tallis Press
Cr. 8vo. 'Poster Reward.' 1905
Illustrated cover. Dated 1905.
Pages 7–224.

B62	FOUR SQUARE JANE.	Readers Library
	Fcp. 8vo. Undated. Pages 9;	1929
	12–186.	
B63	THE FOURTH PLAGUE.	Ward Lock
	Cr. 8vo. Designed cover.	1913
	Illustrated. Dated 1913. Pages	
	5–303; 1–16.	
B64	THE FRIGHTENED LADY.	Hodder &
	Cr. 8vo. Dated. MCMXXXII.	Stoughton
	312 pages.	1932
B65	THE GAUNT STRANGER.	Hodder &
	Cr. 8vo. Undated. Pages 5–320.	Stoughton
	To: My Friend, P. G.	1925
	Wodehouse.	
B66	THE GHOST OF DOWNHILL.	Readers Library
	Fcp. 8vo. Undated. Pages 9–188.	1929
B67	THE GOLDEN HADES.	Collins
	Cr. 8vo. Dated 1929 reverse to	1929
	title page. Illustrated (page	
	251). Pages 5–252.	
B68	GOOD EVANS.	Webster
	Cr. 8vo. Undated. Pages 5–286.	1927
	To: Brownie Carslake. A great	
	Jockey and a good friend.	
B69	THE GOVERNOR OF CHI-FOO.	Newnes
	$8'' \times 5\frac{1}{2}''$ Paperback.	1929
	Illustrated cover. Undated.	
	Pages 5–128.	
B70	THE GREEN ARCHER.	Hodder &
	Cr. 8vo. Undated. Pages v, vi;	Stoughton
	7–318. Dedicated to: Sir	1923
	George Sutton, Bart.	
B71	THE GREEN PACK. (*R. Curtis*)	Hutchinson
	Cr. 8vo. Undated. 288 pages.	1933

B72	THE GREEN RIBBON. Cr. 8vo. Undated. Pages 5–288.	Hutchinson 1929
B73	THE GREEN RUST. Cr. 8vo. Illustrated. Dated 1919. Pages 9–319.	Ward Lock 1919
B74	GREY TIMOTHY. Cr. 8vo. Illustrated cover. Dated 1913. Illustrated. Pages 9–303; 1–16. Dedication to: 'Light Blue and Maize Hoops, Light Blue Cap'.	Ward Lock 1913
B75	THE GUNNER. Cr. 8vo. Dated 1928 reverse to title page. Pages 7–285.	John Long 1928
B76	THE GUV'NOR & OTHER STORIES. Cr. 8vo. dated 1932 reverse to title page. Pages 5; 7–318.	Collins 1932
B77	THE GUV'NOR. $7\frac{1}{4}'' \times 4\frac{1}{2}''$ undated. Pages 7; 9–254.	Collins 1932
B78	THE HAND OF POWER. Cr. 8vo. Dated 1927 reverse to title page and 318. Pages v, vi; 7–318.	John Long 1927
B79	HEROES ALL, GALLANT DEEDS OF THE WAR. Cr. 8vo. Illustrated cover. Illustrated. Undated. Pages 5, 6; 9–255. To the memory of Prince Maurice of Battenberg Kings Royal Rifle Corps who fell whilst gallantly leading his men in France, October 1914.	Newnes 1914

B80   THE INDIA RUBBER MEN.   Hodder &
Cr. 8vo. Undated. Pages 5–312.   Stoughton
Dedicated to: The Hon. Mrs.   1929
James De Rothschild.

B81   THE IRON GRIP.   Readers Library
Fcp. 8vo. Undated. Pages   1930
10, 11; 14–188.

B82   JACK O' JUDGMENT.   Ward Lock
Cr. 8vo. Undated. Pages 6–319   1920

B83   THE JOKER.   Hodder &
Cr. 8vo. Part-illustrated cover. Stoughton
Undated. Pages 5–320.   1926

B84   THE JUST MEN OF CORDOVA.   Ward Lock
Cr. 8vo. Designed cover.   1917
Illustrated. Dated 1917.
Pages 5–303.

B85   KATE PLUS TEN.   Ward Lock
Cr. 8vo. Dated 1919.   1919
Illustrated. Pages 7–304; 1–15.
To: Bryan (B.E.W.)

B86   THE KEEPERS OF THE KINGS   Ward Lock
PEACE.   1917
Cr. 8vo. Designed cover.
Illustrated by Maurice
Grieffenhagen. Dated 1917.
Pages vii; 10–303;
1–16. To Pat: (P.M.C.W.)

B87   KILLER KAY.   Newnes
Paperback. $8\frac{1}{4}'' \times 5\frac{1}{2}''$.   1930
Illustrated cover. Undated.
Pages 5–128.

B88   A KING BY NIGHT.   John Long
Cr. 8vo. Dated 1925 reverse to   1925
title page, and page 320.

Pages 5–320; 1–31. To:
My Friend P.G. Wodehouse.

B89   KITCHENER'S ARMY AND THE   Newnes
TERRITORIAL FORCES.   1915
Large paperback. 11″ × 8″.
Undated. Illustrated cover.
Illustrated. Pages ii, iii, iv;
4–188.

B90   THE LADY CALLED NITA.   Newnes
Paperback. $8\frac{1}{4}″ × 5\frac{1}{2}″$.   1930
Illustrated Cover. Undated.
Pages 7–128.

B91   THE LADY OF ASCOT.   Hutchinson
Cr. 8vo. Undated. Pages 9–288.   1930
Pages (written) two to twenty-
three; twenty-six to thirty-two.

B92   THE LADY OF LITTLE HELL.   Newnes
Paperback. $8\frac{1}{4}″ × 5\frac{1}{2}″$.Undated.   1929
Illustrated cover. Pages 5–127

B93   THE LAST ADVENTURE.   Hutchinson
Cr. 8vo. Undated Pages 11–287;   1934
three to Thirty-eight (written).

B94   THE LAW OF THE FOUR JUST   Hodder &
MEN.   Stoughton
Cr. 8vo. Undated. Pages 7–320.   1921

B95   LIEUTENANT BONES.   Ward Lock
Cr. 8vo. Illustrated cover.   1918
Illustrated by Maurice
Greiffenhagen. Dated 1918.
Pages 5; 7–320.

B96   THE LITTLE GREEN MAN.   Newnes
Paperback. $8\frac{1}{4}″ × 5\frac{1}{2}″$.   1929
Illustrated cover. Undated.
Pages 5–128.

B97 THE LONE HOUSE MYSTERY.   Collins
Cr. 8vo. Dated reverse to title   1929
page 1929. Pages 9–252.

B98 THE MAN AT THE CARLTON.   Hodder &
Cr. 8vo. Undated pages 5–320.   Stoughton
To: Mary Hastings with the   1931
authors love.

B99 THE MAN FROM MOROCCO.   John Long
Cr. 8vo. Dated 1926 reverse to   1926
title page. Pages 7–318.
To: Marney.

B100 THE MAN WHO BOUGHT   Ward Lock
LONDON.   1915
Cr. 8vo. Designed cover.
Illustrated. Dated 1915 reverse to
title page. Pages 6–304; 1–16.

B101 THE MAN WHO CHANGED HIS   Hutchinson
NAME.   1935
Cr. 8vo. Undated. Pages 9–288;
three to forty (written)

B102 THE MAN WHO KNEW.   Newnes
$6\frac{1}{2}'' \times 4''$. Undated. Pages 9;   1919
11–252.

B103 THE MAN WHO WAS NOBODY.   Ward Lock
Cr. 8vo. Dated 1927. Pages   1927
5–256.

B104 THE MELODY OF DEATH.   Arrowsmith/
Cr. 8vo. Dated 1915. Pages   Simpkin Marshall
v, vi; 7–270.

B105 THE MILLION DOLLAR STORY.   Newnes
Paperback $7'' \times 5''$.   1926
Illustrated cover. Undated.
Pages 5–128.

B106 THE MIND OF MR. J. G.   Hodder &
REEDER.   Stoughton
Cr. 8vo. Part cover illustrated.   1925
Undated. Pages 7–319.

B107 THE MISSING MILLION.   John Long
Cr. 8vo. Designed spine.   1923
Dated 1923 reverse to title page.
Pages 7–318. To: The members of
the London Press Club.

B108 THE MISSION THAT FAILED.   T. Maskew Miller
Papercover booklet. 7″ × 5″.   (South Africa)
Illustrated cover. Illustrated.   1898
Photo of Edgar Wallace in Army
Autographed by himself. Dated
reverse to title page 1898.
Pages 6–52. 'This book of verse
is dedicated to W. A. C., an
Uitlander'.

B109 MRS. WILLIAM JONES & BILL.   Newnes
Paperback. 8″ × 5½″.   1930
Illustrated cover. Undated.
Pages 5–128.

B110 MR. J. G. REEDER RETURNS.   Collins
Small Cr. 8vo. Undated.   1934
Pages 7; 9–254.

B111 MR. JUSTICE MAXELL.   Ward Lock
Cr. 8vo. Dated 1922.   1922
Pages 5–303; 1–15.

B112 THE MIXER.   John Long
Cr. 8vo. Dated 1927 reverse to   1927
title page and on 284. Pages
7–284.

B113 MORE EDUCATED EVANS.   Webster
Cr. 8vo. Undated. 288 pages.   1926

B114 THE MOUTHPIECE.   Hutchinson
Cr. 8vo. Undated. Pages 9–304; 1935
two to forty (written).

B115 MY HOLLYWOOD DIARY.   Hutchinson
$8\frac{1}{2}'' \times 5\frac{1}{2}''$. Undated.   1932
Illustrated. Pages 5, 7, 9; 13–259;
one to eighteen (written)

B116 THE NINE BEARS.   Ward Lock
Cr. 8vo. Designed cover.   1910
Illustrated. Dated 1910.
Pages 9–319.

B117 '1925' THE STORY OF A FATAL   Newnes
PEACE.   1915
Stiff paperback. $7'' \times 5''$. Dated
1915. Illustrated cover. Pages
7–128. To: The Creator of
Armies 'K'.

B118 NOBBY.   Newnes
Fcp. 8vo. Designed spine.   1916
Illustrated. Dated 1916. Pages
7–175. Dedication: The
Philistine. Followed by eight
verses of eight lines.

B119 THE NORTHING TRAMP.   Hodder &
Cr. 8vo. Undated. Pages 5–311.   Stoughton
Dedication to Frank Curzon.   1926

B120 NUMBER SIX.   Newnes
Paperback $7'' \times 5''$ Illustrated   1927
cover. Undated. Pages 5; 7–128.

B121 ON THE SPOT   John Long
Cr. 8vo. Undated. 288 pages.   1931

B122 THE ORATOR.   Hutchinson
Cr. 8vo. 288 pages.   1928

B123 PENELOPE OF THE POLYANTHA.   Hodder &
$7'' \times 4\frac{1}{2}''$ Designed cover.   Stoughton
Undated. Pages 5; 7–255.   1926

B124 PEOPLE.   Hodder &
Cr. 8vo. Undated. Pages 5–253.   Stoughton
Dedication: To a Friend of the   1926
People. The Right Hon. The
Earl of Derby K. G.

B125 THE PEOPLE OF THE RIVER.   Ward Lock
Cr. 8vo. Designed cover.   1912
Illustrated. Dated 1912. Pages
9–318; 1–16. Dedication to
Samuel Scott, Bart,. M.P.

B126 PLANETOID 127.   Readers Library
Fcp. 8vo. Undated. Pages 9–252. 1929

B127 THE PRISON BREAKERS.   Newnes
Paperback $8'' \times 5\frac{1}{2}''$. Illustrated   1929
cover. Undated. Pages 5–127.

B128 PRIVATE SELBY.   Ward Lock
Cr. 8vo. Designed cover.   1912
Illustrated. Dated 1912.
Pages 5–303; 1–16.

B129 RED ACES.   Hodder &
Cr. 8vo. Undated. Pages 9–313.   Stoughton
To my friend and Secretary: 1929
R. G. Curtis.

B130 THE REPORTER.   Readers Library
Fcp. 8vo. Undated. Pages   1929
10–254.

B131 THE RIVER OF STARS.   Ward Lock
Cr. 8vo. Illustrated cover.   1913
Illustrated. Dated 1913. Pages
10–303; 1–16. Dedication to:
My sister Gladys Gane.

B132 ROOM 13.   John Long
Cr. 8vo. Designed spine.   1924
Dated 1924 reverse to title page
and on page 318.
Pages 7–318. To: My friend Sir
Emsley Carr KT.

B133 SANCTUARY ISLAND.   Hutchinson
Cr. 8vo. Undated. Pages 5–288; 1936
two to forty (written).

B134 SANDERS.   Hodder &
Cr. 8vo. Undated. Pages 5;   Stoughton
7–317. To: The Mother of   1926
Penelope.

B135 SANDERS OF THE RIVER.   Ward Lock
Cr. 8vo. Illustrated. Dated 1911. 1911
Pages 7–304. Dedication to;
My Brother-in-law, Hugh F.
Griffith, K.C.

B136 SANDI THE KING MAKER.   Ward Lock
Cr. 8vo. Dated 1922. Pages 7;   1922
9–304; 1–16.

B137 THE SECRET HOUSE.   Ward Lock
Cr. 8vo. Designed cover.   1917
Dated 1917. Pages 5–302; 1–15.

B138 SERGEANT SIR PETER.   Chapman & Hall
Cr. 8vo. Designed centre of   1932
cover. Dated reverse to title
page 1932. Pages 9–259.

B139 THE SINISTER MAN.   Hodder &
Cr. 8vo. Undated. Pages v, vi;   Stoughton
7–320. To: 'Babs'.   1924

B140 SMITHY.   Tallis Press
Paperback 7″ × 5″. Illustrated   1905
cover. Dated 1905. Pages 5;

7–128. To: The General whom common people (ignoring rank and title) call French.

B141 SMITHY ABROAD. Hulton
No details known, but a copy is 1909
known to exist in The Bodleian
Library, Oxford, England.

B142 SMITHY & THE HUN. Newnes
Stiff Paperback. 7″ × 5″. 1915
Illustrated cover. Pages 9–157.
Dated 1915.

B143 SMOKY CELL. Hutchinson
Cr. 8vo. Undated. Pages 9–288; 1936
two to forty (written)

B144 THE SQUARE EMERALD. Hodder &
Cr. 8vo. Undated. Pages 5–310. Stoughton
1926

B145 THE SQUEAKER. Hodder &
Cr. 8vo. Undated. Pages 5–312. Stoughton
To: Margaret Penelope June. 1927

B146 STANDARD HISTORY OF THE WAR. Newnes
All four vols. Fcp. 8vo. 1914
Illustrated. Undated.
Vol. 1. Pages v, vi; 7–159.
Vol. 2. Pages v, vi; 7–160.
Vol. 3. Pages 2–160.
Vol. 4. Pages 5; 7–159.

B147 THE STEWARD. Collins
Cr. 8vo. Dated 1932 reverse to 1932
title page. Pages 5; 7–252.

B148 THE STRANGE COUNTESS. Hodder &
Cr. 8vo. Illustrated part cover. Stoughton
Undated. Pages 11–320. To: 1925
D. C. Thomson with the author's

happiest memories of a long
business association.

B149 THE TABLE.   Hutchinson
Cr. 8vo. Undated. Pages 5–287; 1936
three to forty (written).

B150 TAM OF THE SCOUTS.   Newnes
Cr. 8vo. Illustrated cover.   1918
Illustrated by Scott Calder.
Dated 1918. Pages 13–287.
To: K. J.

B151 THE TERRIBLE PEOPLE.   Hodder &
Cr. 8vo. Part illustrated cover.   Stoughton
Undated. Pages 5–308; 1–4.   1926
To: C. E. Alexander Macleod,
F.R.C.S. (Eng), in all affection.

B152 THE TERROR.   Collins
Fcp. 8vo. Illustrated cover.   1929
Undated. Pages 7–190.

B153 TERROR KEEP.   Hodder &
Cr. 8vo. Undated. Pages 6–312.   Stoughton
To: 'Leslie Faber'.   1927

B154 THE THIEF IN THE NIGHT.   Readers Library
Fcp. 8vo. Undated. Pages 9, 10;   1928
12–183.

B155 THIS ENGLAND.   Hodder &
Cr. 8vo. Illustrated. Undated.   Stoughton
Pages vii; 13–247. Dedication: 1927
These little bits of observation
and experience, are reprinted
from the '*Morning Post*'. They
might be pretentiously and
truthfully entitled leaves from a
journalists notebook, but I
refrain! With all their

imperfections I dedicate them to master writer of our amusing trade.

Rudyard Kipling.

B156 THOSE FOLK OF BULBORO. Ward Lock
Cr. 8vo. Illustrated. Dated 1918. 1918
Pages 6–304; 1–16.

B157 THE THREE JUST MEN. Hodder &
Cr. 8vo. Undated. 316 pages. Stoughton
1926

B158 THE THREE OAK MYSTERY. Ward Lock
Cr. 8vo. Dated 1924. Pages 1924
12–317.

B159 THE TOMB OF T'SIN. Ward Lock
Cr. 8vo. Designed cover. 1916
Illustrated. Dated 1916. Pages
7–303; 1–16.

B160 THE TRAITORS GATE. Hodder &
Cr. 8vo. Undated. Pages 5–312. Stoughton
To: My dear friend Dorothy 1927
Dickson ('Cora Ann').

B161 THE TWISTER. John Long
Cr. 8vo Dated 1928 reverse to 1928
title page. Pages 5–288.

B162 THE UNDISCLOSED CLIENT. Digit Books
$7'' \times 4\frac{1}{4}''$. Paperback. 1963
Illustrated cover. Undated.
Pages 5–159.

B163 UNOFFICIAL DISPATCHES. Hutchinson
Cr. 8vo. Illustrated. Undated. 1901
Pages viii; 10–327. Dedicated to:
Lieutenant-Colonel the Hon.
Arthur Henniker, C.B. 2nd
Coldstream Guards.

B164 THE VALLEY OF GHOSTS.
Cr. 8vo. No other details
available.

Odhams
1922

B165 WAR AND OTHER POEMS.
$8\frac{1}{4}'' \times 5\frac{1}{4}''$. Paperback booklet.
Undated. Pages 4–10.

Eastern Press
(South Africa)
1900

B166 WAR OF THE NATIONS.
Vols. 2–11. $13'' \times 10''$. Red
cloth with pictures of soldiers
and sailors on covers. (No other
details available).

Newnes
1915/17

B167 WE SHALL SEE.
Small Cr. 8vo. Designed cover.
Undated. Pages 5; 7–255.

Hodder &
Stoughton
1926

B168 WHEN THE GANGS CAME TO
LONDON.
Cr. 8vo. Undated. Pages 10–288;
2–32.

John Long
1932

B169 WHITE FACE.
Cr. 8vo. Dated MCMXXX.
Pages 5–312. Dedicated to my
dear friend George Doran.

Hodder &
Stoughton
1930

B170 THE WOMAN FROM THE EAST.
Cr. 8vo. Undated. Pages xi to
xviii; 21–287; three to forty-
eight (written).

Hutchinson
1934

B171 WRIT IN BARRACKS.
$7'' \times 5''$. Dated 1900. Pages ix,
x; 1–120; 3–47. Dedicated to
the rank and file of the Royal
Army Medical Corps amongst
whom I spent six happy years of
my life—this collection of
verses, mostly written in

Methuen
1900

barracks is admiringly
dedicated.

B172   THE YELLOW SNAKE.   Hodder &
Cr. 8vo. Part illustrated cover.   Stoughton
Undated. Pages 5–318. To: 1926
Arthur Moreland.

Notes

1. Pages given are those exactly numbered by publishers, and includes their own errors.
2. The Hodder & Stoughton copies given as undated are completely undated in any form whatsoever. Readers who may have copies e.g. 'First printed 1926' on the reverse to the title page, do not have the actual first edition.
3. B89. It has been established that a de-luxe edition of this was published in the publishers own special binding and issued simultaneously with the first ordinary issue. It is quite possible that other 'Newnes' similar publications were issued this way.
4. B118. The earlier edition of this work since discovered entitled 'Smithy's Friend Nobby' has the following details:
   Paperback. Illustrated cover.
   $7\frac{1}{4}'' \times 5''$. Dated 1914.
   Illustrated by G. M. Payne.
   Pages 7–172.

THE WORKS OF EDGAR WALLACE PUBLISHED IN BOOK FORM

Abbreviations

A	American Title (used only where similarity might otherwise cause confusion).
V	Verse.
HF	Historical Fiction.
NF	Non Fiction.
SS	Short stories with central character.
CSS	Collected (misc.) short stories.
LSS	Long short stories.
BK	Book.
MG	Magazine.
N	Newspaper.
EWMM	Edgar Wallace Mystery Magazine.

All stories have opening words of chapter in brackets.

SS **B1** **Admirable Carfew, The**
Ward Lock & Co. 1914
Ward Lock 6d Copyright Novels 224

CARFEW 11 (It was an idea; even Jenkins . . .)
MG *Windsor Magazine*, Vol. 34, June to Nov. 1911. Carfew 11.

CARFEW, WITHINGTON & CO., INVENTORS (Carfew could never quite . . .)
MG *Windsor Magazine*, Vol. 35, Dec. 1911 to May 1912. Carfew Withington & Co., Inventors.

THE AGREEABLE COMPANY (A man who attracted money . . .)
MG *Windsor Magazine*, Vol. 36, June to Nov. 1912. The Agreeable Company.

CARFEW IS ADVISED (He was young and he was rich . . .)

MG   *Windsor Magazine*, Vol. 36, June to Nov. 1912. Carfew is Advised.

A DEAL IN RIFFS (It was in his house in . . .)

MG   *Windsor Magazine*, Vol. 37, Dec. 1912 to May 1913. A Deal in Riffs.

CARFEW ENTERTAINS (Very few people know the truth . . .)

MG   *Windsor Magazine*, Vol. 37, Dec. 1912 to May 1913. Carfew Entertains.

THE ECCENTRIC MR. GOBLEHEIM (It is the the truth that Carfew . . .)

MG   *Windsor Magazine*, Vol. 37, Dec. 1912 to May 1913. The Eccentric Mr. Gobleheim.

*PATRIOTS (You must remember about Carfew . . .)

    Windsor Magazine, Vol. 38. June to Nov. 1913.

TOBBINS, LIMITED (Mr. Carfew's broker called him up . . .)

MG   *Windsor Magazine*, Vol. 38, June to Nov. 1913. Tobbins, Limited.

CARFEW—IMPRESARIO (A thousand pounds is a lot . . .)

MG   *Windsor Magazine*, Vol. 39, Dec. 1913 to May 1914. Carfew—Impresario.

CARFEW PRODUCES (There is an uninteresting part to . . .)

MG   *Windsor Magazine*, Vol. 39, Dec. 1913 to May 1914. Carfew Produces.

WHY GELDEN MADE A MILLION (In the days when Carfew was . . .)

*Rewritten and published in THE WOMAN FROM THE EAST.

MG   *Windsor Magazine*, Vol. 39, Dec. 1913 to May 1914. Why Gelden made a million.

CARFEW AND THE 'MARY Q' (What kindness of heart was . . .)

MG   *Windsor Magazine*, Vol. 39, Dec. 1913 to May 1914. Carfew and the 'Mary Q'.

A MATTER OF BUSINESS (Only Carfew knows whether he was . . .)

MG   *Windsor Magazine*, Vol. 40, June to Nov. 1914. A Matter of Business.

ONE AND SEVENPENCE HA'PENNY (Carfew sat in his study . . .)

MG   *Windsor Magazine*, Vol. 40, June to Nov. 1914. One and Sevenpence Ha'penny.

SS   B2   **Adventures of Heine, The**
Ward Lock & Co. 1919, 1924, 1930.
Wardlock 6d. Copyright Novels 285.

ALEXANDER & THE LADY (Secret Service work is a joke . . .)
THE MAN WHO DWELT ON A HILL (When I left London hurriedly . . .)
THE LOVELY MISS HARRYMORE (In America, where German . . .)
THE AFFAIR OF MISTER HAYES (In February 1915 . . .)
THE MAN FROM THE STARS (In the summer of 1915 . . .)
THE AFFAIR OF THE ALLIED CONFERENCE (I think it must have been . . .)
THE WORD OF A PRINCE (There is a moral in . . .)

THE JERMYN CREDIT BANK (When I came to England . . .)

MR. COLLINGREY M.P. PACIFIST (I have often said . . .)

THE GREY ENVELOPE (It was in 1917 . . .)

THE MURDERERS (In the latter days of March 1915 . . .)

THE PASSING OF HEINE (The British people . . .)

THE U BOAT ADVENTURE (As I stood on the broad deck . . .)

BRETHREN OF THE ORDER (Consider dear friends . . .)

THE WORLD DICTATOR (I pass to the strangest adventure . . .)

THE SYREN (I have mentioned in an earlier chapter . . .)

THE COMING OF THE BOLSHEVIKS (If there is one quality . . .)

THE GOING OF HEINE (Picture my feelings . . .)

SS   **B3**   **Again Sanders**
Hodder & Stoughton 1928.
Hodder & Stoughton 9d Yellow Jackets.
Pan Books 1961, 1963.

BONES AND THE BEE (MaKara, chief of Kobala'ba was . . .)
MG   Presumed *Grand Magazine*.

THE TERRIBLE TALKER (There was a man of the Isisi . . .)
MG   Presumed *Grand Magazine*.

THY NEIGHBOUR AS THYSELF (There was once an earnest . . .)

MG		Presumed *Grand Magazine*.

THE GHOST WALKER (Don Murdock came to the . . .)

MG   Presumed *Grand Magazine*.

THE KING'S SCEPTRE (Breakfast time was the hour . . .)

MG   Presumed *Grand Magazine*.

IN THE MANNER OF LIPSTICK (It was one of those glorious . . .)

MG   Presumed *Grand Magazine*.

THE SPLENDID THINGS (The two splendid things . . .)

MG   *Grand Magazine*, Vol. 49, Mar to Aug. 1926. Bones Falls in Love.

BONES THE PSYCHIC (Miss Caroline Tibbets was a lady . . .)

MG   Presumed *Grand Magazine*.

THE RICH WOMAN (There was a gentleman in New York . . .)

MG   Presumed *Grand Magazine*.

THE KEEPERS OF THE TREASURE (Years and years ago . . .)

MG   Presumed *Grand Magazine*.

THE PRESENT (D'Mini, the dancing girl . . .)

MG   Presumed *Grand Magazine*.

M'GALA THE ACCURST (Once upon a time a secretary . . .)

MG   Presumed *Grand Magazine*.

SS   **B4**   **Again the Ringer** (Alt. title: The Ringer Returns)

Hodder & Stoughton, March 1929, April 1949, Aug. 1952, 1957, Pan Books 1961, 1962.

THE MAN WITH THE RED BEARD (To the average reader . . .)

CASE OF THE HOME SECRETARY (There are two schools of . . .)

THE MURDERER OF MANY NAMES (Mr. Ellroyd arrived in England . . .)

A SERVANT OF WOMEN (Once upon a time, in those absurd . . .)

THE TRIMMING OF PAUL LUMIERE (It is not for me, sir, ever to . . .)

THE BLACKMAIL BOOMERANG (There was a man who had an office . . .)

MISS BROWN'S £7,000 WINDFALL (Mr. Gilbert Orsan was an . . .)

THE END OF MR. BASH—THE BRUTAL ('Bash' was really clever . . .)

THE COMPLETE VAMPIRE (There was a skid on the road . . .)

THE SWISS HEAD WAITER (There was a broad streak . . .)

THE ESCAPE OF MR. BLISS (There was an incident on . . .)

THE MAN WITH THE BEARD (The trouble with Mr. Bliss . . .)

THE ACCIDENTAL SNAPSHOT (People have the most unlikely . . .)

THE SINISTER DR. LUTTEUR (Inspector Mander had a great . . .)

THE OBLIGING COBBLER (Doctors are credited with . . .)

THE FORTUNE OF FORGERY (The man who reclined . . .)

MG   *Saint Mag.* (Br.) Oct. 1960. The Fortune of Forgery.

A 'YARD' MAN KIDNAPPED (Government Departments keep a sharp . . .)

Again the Three (See **B5**)

SS   **B5**   **Again the Three Just Men** (Alt. title: Again the Three) (A. The Law of the The Three Just Men)

*Hodder & Stoughton March 1928, 1952.
Hodder & Stoughton 9d. Yellow Jackets.

THE REBUS (As the Megaphone once said . . .)
THE HAPPY TRAVELLERS (Of the three men who had . . .)

MG   *Saint Mag.* (Br.) Apr. 1959 The Happy Travellers.

THE ABDUCTOR (It was just a year since . . .)
THE THIRD COINCIDENCE (Leon Gonsalez, like the famous . . .)
THE SLANE MYSTERY (The killing of Bernard Slane . . .)

MG   *Saint Mag.* (Br.), July 1962. The Slane Mystery.

THE MARKED CHEQUE (The man who called at the . . .)
MR. LEVINGRON'S DAUGHTER (Mr. Levingron took his long cigar . . .)
THE SHARE PUSHER (The man whom Raymond Poiccart . . .

MG   *John Bull Xmas Annual* 1927: The Share Pusher.

THE MAN WHO SANG IN CHURCH (To Leon Gonsalez went most of the . . .)

*Note: Some Editions Also Contained Fourteen Cablegrams.

MG		*Saint Mag.* (Br.), Feb. 1959. The Man who Sang in Church.
MG		20 *Story Magazine*, Sept. 1927. The Man who Sang in Church.
		THE LADY FROM BRAZIL (The journey had begun in a . . .)
MG		20 *Story Magazine*, Oct. 1927. The Lady from Brazil.
		THE TYPIST WHO SAW THINGS (About every six months . . .)
MG		20 *Story Magazine*, Nov. 1927. The Typist who saw things.
		THE MYSTERY OF MR. DRAKE (All events go in threes . . .)
MG		20 *Story Magazine*, Dec. 1927. The Mystery of Mr. Drake.
		THE ENGLISHMAN KONNER (The Three Just Men sat longer . . .)
MG		*Saint Mag.* (Br.), Nov. 1960. The Englishman Konner.
MG		20 *Story Magazine*, Jan. 1928. The Englishman Konner.

A		**Again the Three Just Men**
	B6	**Angel Esquire** (Mr. William Spedding, of the firm of . . .) Joint Publishers: J. W. Arrowsmith/, Simpkin Marshall, Bristol 1908, 1925, 1927, 1928, 1930. Macdonald (Date unknown). Readers Library 1928, 1939, Tallis Press 1966. Queensway Library 1929.
MG		*Ideas*, 149–157, 25 Jan. to 18 Mar. 1908.

MG

Angel Esquire.
Edgar Wallace Mystery Magazine (Br.), 17–20
Angel Esquire.

B7   **Angel of Terror, The** (The hush of the court which had . . .)
Hodder & Stoughton 1922.
Hodder & Stoughton 9d. Yellow Jackets.
Pan Books 1959, 1962.

MG

Ideas, 1037–1049, 17 Jan. to 11 Apr. 1925. The Angel of Terror.

Arranways Mystery, The (See **B32**)

B8   **Avenger, The** (Alt. titles: The Hairy Arm & The Extra Girl) (Captain Mike Brixan had certain mild . . .) John Long 1926, June 1927, Aug. 1927, 1928, cheap ed. 1928, 1929, 1929, 1930, 1931, 1932, 1937, Jan. 1949. Leisure Library 1929, Arrow 1962, F. A. Thorpe 1964.

B9   **Barbara on her Own** (On that day of fate, when, it seemed, . . .)
Newnes (1) 1926; (2) 1926; (3) 1926; (4) 1927; (5) 1928; new size novels 1928. C. A. Ransom & Co. Paper Covered edition.

Beyond Recall (see **B15**)

B10   **Big Foot** (It was a coincidence that Sooper . . .)
Features Superintendent Minter.
Leisure Library, not dated.
John Long 1927; Cherry Tree Books No. 16, 1938; Arrow.

44

SS   **B11**   **Big Four, The** (Alt. title: Crooks of Society)
Readers Library 1929.

The Big Four Syndicate and The Man Who
Smashed It (To all outward appearance . . .)

MG   *E.W.M.M.* (Br.), 6 Jan. 1965. The Boss of the
Big Four.

The Burglary at Goodwood (Bob Brewer,
temporary chief of . . .)

MG   *E.W.M.M.* (Br.), 24 Jul. 1966. The Burglary
at Goodwood.

Baccarat at Cowes (When Henry B.
Vandersluis determined . . .)
A Race at Ostend (What do people go to
Ostend . . .)

The Heppleworth Pearls (Lord Heppleworth looked over his . . .)

MG   *E.W.M.M.* (Br.), 12 Jul. 1965. Mutation in
Pearls.

'Pinky' and the Bank Manager (Bob
Brewer was eating his . . .)
The Star of the World (Mr. Douglas
Campbell, that eminent . . .)
Bob Brewer's biggest Coup (You can say
what you like . . .)

SS   **B12**   **Black, The** (Alt. title: Blackmailers I have
foiled)
Features Superintendant Minter.
Readers Library 1929; Digit 1962.

The Case of Lady Purseyence (Two years
ago I received . . .)

THE WIFE OF SIR RALPH CRETAPACE (It was time that conscience)

THE CASE OF MRS. ANTHONY STRATMORE (One of the most extraordinary . . .)

THE MYSTERY OF THE BISHOP'S CHAIR (Turning over a file of . . .)

THE TWENTY THOUSAND POUND KISS (Of all the cases I have had . . .)

HOW A CROOK SPOOFED ANOTHER CROOK (If you were to ask me . . .)

A DOCTOR'S JOLLIFICATION AND ITS SEQUEL (I will now tell you the story . . .)

THE MILLIONAIRE'S SECRET (Mrs. Middleton returning to her . . .)

*WARM AND DRY (I went down to see the Superintendant . . .)

MG   *E.W.M.M.* (Br.), 32 Mar. 1967. Warm & Dry.

*THE SOOPER SPEAKING (It was a queer thing said the . . .)

A   **Black, The** (see **B99**)

B13   **Black Abbot, The** (Thomas! Yes M'Lord . . .)
Hodder & Stoughton, Apr. 1926, 1941, 1950.
Hodder & Stoughton 9d. Yellow Jackets.

MG   *Answers*, 1950–1966, 10 Oct. 1925 to 30 Jan. 1926. The Second Son.

HF   **B14**   **Black Avons, The**
G. Gill & Sons 1925, 4 vols.

*In Digit edition only.

How they Fared in the times of the
Tudors (I begin by setting forth. . . .)
Roundhead and Cavalier (If in this narra-
tive pertaining to. . . .)
From Waterloo to the Mutiny (Into what
a troubled world I . . .)
Europe in the Melting Pot (It is almost in-
conceivable that. . .)

Blackmailers I have Foiled (see **B12**)

Black Tenth, The (see **B172**)

B15 **Blue Hand, The** (Alt. title: Beyond Recall)
(Mr. Septimus Salter pressed the bell . . .)
Ward Lock & Co., 1925, 1956. Digit 1963.
Ward Lock 6d. Copyright Novels.

MG *Answers*, 1743–1769, 22 Oct. 1921–22 Apr.
1922. Beyond Recall.
Under name of Richard Cloud.

SS **B16** **Bones**
Ward Lock & Co. 1915.
Ward Lock 6d. Copyright Novels 220.
Digit 1963.

Sanders—C. M. G. (You will never know
from . . .)
MG *Weekly Tale Teller*, 284, 10 Oct. 1914.
Sanders—C. M. G.

Hamilton of the Houssas (Sanders turned to
the rail . . .)
MG *Weekly Tale Teller*, 285, 17 Oct. 1914 The
Advent of Bones.

THE DISCIPLINARIANS (Lieutenant Augustus Tibbetts of the Houssas stood . . .)

MG   *Weekly Tale Teller*, 286, 24 Oct. 1914. The Disciplinarians.

THE LOST N'BOSINI (Militani, there is a bad palaver . . .)

MG   *Weekly Tale Teller*, 287, 31 Oct. 1914. The Lost N'Bosini.

THE FETISH STICK (N'Gori the chief had a son who . . .)

MG   *Weekly Tale Teller*, 288, 7 Nov. 1914. The Fetish Stick.

THE FRONTIER AND A CODE (To understand this story . . .)

MG   *Weekly Tale Teller*, 289, 14 Nov. 1914. The Frontier and a Code.

THE SOUL OF A NATIVE WOMAN (Mail day is ever a day of . . .)

MG   **Weekly Tale Teller*, 290, 21 Nov. 1914. The Book of Bones.

THE STRANGER WHO WALKED BY NIGHT (Since the day when Lieutenant . . .)

MG   **Weekly Tale Teller*, 296, 2 Jan. 1915. The Stranger who Walked by Night.

A RIGHT OF WAY (The borders of territories may be fixed . . .)

MG   **Weekly Tale Teller*, 295, 26 Dec. 1914. A Right of Way.

THE GREEN CROCODILE (Cala Cala, as they say, seven . . .)

*Stories printed out of sequence in book.

MG   *Weekly Tale Teller*, 294, 19 Dec. 1914. The Green Crocodile.

HENRY HAMILTON BONES (Lieutenant Francis Augustus Tibbetts of the Houssas . . .)

MG   *Weekly Tale Teller*, 293, 12 Dec. 1914. Henry Hamilton Bones.

BONES AT M'FA (Hamilton of the Houssas coming down to . . .)

MG   *Weekly Tale Teller*, 291, 28 Nov. 1914. Bones at M'Fa.

THE MAN WHO DID NOT SLEEP. (No doubt whatever but that . . .)

MG   *Weekly Tale Teller*, 292, 5 Dec. 1914. The Man who did not Sleep.

B17   **Bones in London**
Ward Lock & Co. 1921

BONES & BIG BUSINESS (There was a slump in . . .)

MG   *Windsor Magazine*, Vol. 51, Dec. 1919 to May 1920. Bones & Big Business.

HIDDEN TREASURE (Mrs. Staleyborn's first Husband. . . .)

MG   *Windsor Magazine*, Vol. 51, Dec. 1919 to May 1920. Hidden Treasure.

BONES & THE WHARFINGERS (The kite wheeling invisible . . .)

MG   *Windsor Magazine*, Vol. 51, Dec. 1919 to May 1920. Bones & the Wharfingers.

THE PLOVER-LIGHT CAR (The door of the private office . . .)

MG   *Windsor Magazine*, Vol. 51, Dec. 1919 to May 1920. The Light-Plover Car.

*Stories printed out of sequence in book.

A CINEMA PICTURE (Mr. Augustus Tibbetts called Bones . . .)

MG   *Windsor Magazine*, Vol. 51, Dec. 1919 to May 1920. A Cinema Picture.

A DEAL IN JUTE (It is a reasonable theory . . .)

MG   *Windsor Magazine*, Vol. 51, Dec. 1919 to May 1920. A Deal in Jute.

DETECTIVE BONES (Mr. Harold de Vinne was a . . .)

MG   *Windsor Magazine*, Vol. 52, June to Nov. 1920. Detective Bones.

COMPETENT JUDGE OF POETRY (There were times when Mr. Cresta Morris . . .)

MG   *Windsor Magazine*, Vol. 52, Jun. to Nov. 1920. A Competent Judge of Poetry.

THE LAMP THAT NEVER WENT OUT (Have you seen her asked Bones . . .)

MG   *Windsor Magazine*, Vol. 52, June to Nov. 1920. The Lamp that Never Went Out.

THE BRANCH LINE (Not all the investments of Bones . . .)

MG   *Windsor Magazine*, Vol. 52, June to Nov. 1920. The Branch Line.

A STUDENT OF MEN (Mr. Jackson Hyane was one . . .)

MG   *Windsor Magazine*, Vol. 52, June to Nov. 1920. A Student of Men.

BONES HITS BACK (It may be said of Bones . . .)

MG   *Windsor Magazine*, Vol. 52, June to Nov. 1920. Bones Hits Back.

SS   **B18**   **Bones of the River**
George Newnes 1923, 1924, 1926, 1928, 1935.
C. A. Ransom & Co. Paper Covered Edition.

THE FEARFUL WORD (Look after the chickens . . .)

MG   20 *Story Magazine*, Nov. 1922. The Fearful Word.

THE MEDICAL OFFICER OF HEALTH (For the use of Mr. Augustus Tibbetts . . .)

MG   20 *Story Magazine*, March 1923. The Medical Officer of Health.

THE BLACK EGG (Once upon a time in the Isisi Land . . .)

MG   20 *Story Magazine*, Feb. 1923. The Black Egg.

A NICE GEL (Because Terence Doughty . . .)

MG   20 *Story Magazine*, Jan. 1923. A Nice Gel.

THE BRASS BEDSTEAD (There is no tribe in the river . . .)

MG   20 *Story Magazine*, April 1923. The Brass Bedstead.

A LOVER OF DOGS (The mail boat had come into sight . . .)

MG   20 *Story Magazine*, Dec. 1922. A Lover of Dogs.

THE CAMERA MAN (For a thousand years . . .)

MG   20 *Story Magazine*, May 1923. The Camera Man.

THE HEALER (Men lie with a certain transparent . . .)

MG   20 *Story Magazine*, Aug. 1923. The Healer.

THE WAZOOS (When Bones brushed his hair . . .)

MG   20 *Story Magazine*, July 1923. The Wazoos.

THE ALL-AFRICANS (The mind of Mr. Commissioner Sanders . . .)

MG   20 *Story Magazine*, June 1923. The All Africans.

THE WOMAN WHO SPOKE TO BIRDS (There was a man named . . .)

MG   20 *Story Magazine*, Sept. 1923. The Woman who spoke to Birds.

THE LAKE OF THE DEVIL (M'Suru an Akasava Chief . . .)

MG   20 *Story Magazine*, Oct. 1923. The Lake of the Devil.

B19   **Book of all Power, The** (If a man is not eager for adventure . . .)
Ward Lock & Co. 1921, 1924.
Ward Lock 6d. Copyright novels 249.

B20   **Books of Bart, The**
Ward Lock & Co. 1923, 1927.

THE BOOK OF ARRANGEMENT (Everybody agreed that a man . . .)
THE BOOK OF ADJUSTMENT (Mr. Packer had time to look . . .)
THE BOOK OF DEVELOPMENT (Bart sat hunched up in . . .)
THE BOOK OF ENLIGHTMENT (Bart shut the long French . . .)

SS   **B21**   **Bosambo of the River**
Ward Lock & Co. 1914; Digit 1963.

ARACHI THE BORROWER (Many years ago the Monrovian . . .)

MG   *Weekly Tale Teller*, 197, 8 Feb. 1913. Arachi the Borrower.

MG   *Chums*, 1927–8. Arachi the Borrower.

THE TAX RESISTORS (Sanders took nothing for granted . . .)

MG   *Weekly Tale Teller*, 201, 8 Mar. 1913. The Tax Resistors.

MG   *Chums*, 1927–8. The Tax Resistors.

THE RISE OF THE EMPEROR (Tobolaka, the King of the Isisi . . .)

MG   *Weekly Tale Teller*, 206, 12. 1913. The Rise of the Emperor.

MG   *Chums*, 1927–8. The Rise of the Emperor.

THE FALL OF THE EMPEROR (My poor soul! said the Houssa . . .)

MG   *Chums*, 1927–8. The Fall of the Emperor.

MG   *Weekly Tale Teller*, 207, 19 Apr. 1913. The Fall of Tobolaka.

THE KILLING OF OLANDI (Chief of Sanders spies . . .)

MG   *Weekly Tale Teller*, 213, 31 May 1913. The Killing of Olandi.

MG   *Chums*, 1927–8. The Killing of Olandi.

THE PEDOMETER (Bosambo, the chief of the Ochori . . .)

MG   *Weekly Tale Teller*, 226, 30 Aug. 1913. The Pedometer.

MG   *Chums*, 1927–8. The Pedometer.

THE BROTHER OF BOSAMBO (Bosambo was a Monrovian . . .)

MG   *Chums*, 1927–8. The Brother of Bosambo.

MG   *Weekly Tale Teller*, 238, 22 Nov. 1913 King of the Ochori.

THE CHAIR OF THE N'GOMBI (The N'Gombi people prized . . .)

MG   *Weekly Tale Teller*, 239, 29 Nov. 1913. The Chair of the N'Gombi.

MG   *Chums*, 1927–8. The Chair of the N'Gombi.

THE KI-CHU (The messenger from Sakola . . .)

MG   *Weekly Tale Teller*, 240, 6 Dec. 1913. The Ki-Chu.

MG   *Chums*, 1927–8. The Ki-Chu.

THE CHILD OF SACRIFICE (Out of the waste came a long . . .)

MG   *Weekly Tale Teller*, 241, 13 Dec. 1913. The Wonderful Lover.

MG   *Chums*, 1927–8. The Child of Sacrifice.

'THEY' (In the Akarti country they . . .)

MG   *Weekly Tale Teller*, 242, 20 Dec. 1913. 'They'.

MG   *Chums*, 1927–8. 'They'.

THE AMBASSADORS (There is a saying amongst the . . .)

MG   *Chums*, 1927–8. The Ambassadors.

     Weekly Tale Teller, 243, 27 Dec. 1913. Bosambo's Devils.

GUNS IN THE AKASAVA (Thank God! said the Houssa . . .)

MG   *Chums*, 1927–8. Guns in the Akasava.

SS   **B22**   **Brigand, The**
Hodder & Stoughton 1927. Hodder & Stoughton 9d. Yellow Jackets; Pan Books 1964.

A MATTER OF NERVE (Anthony Newton was a soldier . . .)

MG   *Thriller*, 337, 20 July 1935. The Nerve of Tony Newton.

ON GETTING AN INTRODUCTION (Polite brigandage has its novel . . .)

BURIED TREASURE (Mr. Tony Newton threw up the window . . .)

A CONTRIBUTION TO CHARITY (Tony Newton was not given to . . .)

THE LADY IN GREY (During the hectic days of war . . .)

ANTHONY THE BOOKMAKER (Human nature said Anthony Newton . . .)

MG *Thriller*, 344, 7 Sept. 1935. Tony Newton Bookmaker.

THE PLUM PUDDING GIRL (No man said Tony Newton . . .)

THE GUEST OF THE MINNOWS (Tony Newton was strong in . . .)

MG *Novel Magazine*, Jan. 1923. The Guest of the Minnows.

THE BURSTED ELECTION (In the centuries ahead . . .)

MG *Thriller*, 357, 7 Dec. 1935. Vote for Tony Newton.

MG *Novel Magazine*, Feb. 1923. The Bursted Election.

THE JOKER (Mr. Anthony Newton had enjoyed . . .)

MG *Thriller*, 358, 14 Dec. 1935. The Joke of a Lifetime.

MG *Novel Magazine*, Mar. 1923, The Joker.

KATO (Brigandage Mr. Newton admitted . . .)

THE GRAFT (Tony Newton was an opportunist . . .)

MG *Novel Magazine*, Apr. 1923. Crooked Dealings.

B23 **Calendar, The** (Do you like me well enough to let . . .)
Collins 1930, 1932; Pan Books 1961.
Play: Frenchs Acting Edition 1932–3 acts.

B24 **Captains of Souls** (Beryl Merville wrote . . .)
Hutchinson 1923; John Long 1923, 1924;
Arrow 1961; Cherry Tree Books No. 18 1938.

B25 **Captain Tatham of Tatham Island** (Alt. titles: Eve's Island; The Island of Galloping Gold). (Edward G. Tatham was born in . . .)
Gale & Polden 1909.

Case of the Frightened Lady, The (see B64)

CSS **B26** **Cat Burglar, The**
George Newnes 1929.

All stories reprinted in Forty Eight Short Stories.

THE CAT BURGLAR (Old Tom Burkes used to say . . .)

BK   Digit. The Terror: The Cat Burglar.

THE PICK UP (It was the day before . . .)

MG   *John Bull Summer Annual*, 1927. The Pick Up.

DISCOVERING REX (In the office of the Public Prosecutor . . .)

THE KNOW HOW. (What you need Dian . . .)

WHITE STOCKING (John Trevor was not a jealous man . . .)

MG   *Thriller*, 312, 26 Jan. 1935. White Stocking.
Grand Magazine, Vol. 41, March to Aug. 1922. White Stocking.

N   *Evening Standard*, 6 June 1934. White Stocking.

THE CLUE OF MONDAY'S SETTLING (It did not seem possible to . . .)

MG   *E.W.W.M.* (Br.), 8 Mar. 1965. The Clue of Mondays Settling.

BK   *Fifty Masterpieces of Mystery*. The Clue of Mondays Settling.

ESTABLISHING CHARLES BULLIVANT (There's a new doctor . . .)

SENTIMENTAL SIMPSON (According to certain signs . . .)

MG   *E.W.M.M.* (Br.), 7 Feb. 1965. The Fall of Sentimental Simpson.

MG   *Happy Mag.*, 1 June 1922. The Sentimental Crook.

Cheaters, The Alt. Title: (The Nine Bears). Digit 1964.

SS   **B27**   **Chick**
Ward Lock & Co. 1923, 1929.
Ward Lock 6d. Copyright novels 245.

CHICK (Mr. Jonas Stollingham . . .)

MG   *Windsor Magazine*, Vol. 55, Dec. 1921 to May 1922. Chick.

FOR ONE NIGHT ONLY ('Good morning', said Chick . . .)

MG   *Windsor Magazine*, Vol. 55, Dec. 1921 to May 1922. For One Night Only.

A WRIT OF SUMMONS (Had the eminent author . . .)

MG   *Windsor Magazine*, Vol. 55, Dec. 1921 to May 1922. A Writ of Summons.

SPOTTING THE LADY (Lord Pelborough (C.U.) . . .)

CHICK, WAITER (Gwenda Maynard . . .)

MG   *Windsor Magazine*, Vol. 55, Dec. 1921 to May 1922. Chick, Waiter.

A LESSON IN DIPLOMACY (The Most Honourable . . .)

MG   *Windsor Magazine*, Vol. 55, Dec. 1921 to May 1922. A Lesson in Diplomacy.

THE FIRST DISPATCH (The Marquis of Pelborough . . .)

MG   *Windsor Magazine*, Vol. 55, Dec. 1921 to May 1922. The First Dispatch.

THE OILFIELD ('No, thank you, Joicey' . . .)

MG   *Windsor Magazine*, Vol. 56, June to Nov. 1922. The Oilfield.

IN THE PUBLIC EYE (Sudden Affluence . . .)

MG   *Windsor Magazine*, Vol. 56, June to Nov. 1922. In the Public Eye.

COURAGE (The beauty of Monte Carlo . . .)

MG   *Windsor Magazine*, Vol. 56, June to Nov. 1922 Courage.

THE MAN FROM TOULOUSE (When Jagg Flower . . .)

MG   *Windsor Magazine*, Vol. 56, June to Nov. 1922. The Man from Toulouse.

THE BEATING OF THE MIDDLE-WEIGHT (There is a sixth sense . . .)

MG   *Windsor Magazine*, Vol. 56, June to Nov. 1922. The Beating of the Middle-Weight.

Children of the Poor (see **B75**)

CSS   **B28**   **Circumstantial Evidence**
George Newnes 1929.
All stories reprinted in Forty Eight Short Stories.

Circumstantial Evidence (Colonel Chartres Dane lingered . . .)

BK   *Black Cap*. Circumstantial Evidence.

MG   *Strand Magazine*, Aug. 1922. Circumstantial Evidence.

MG   *E.W.M.M.* (Br.), No. 9, Apr. 1965. Circumstantial Evidence.

The Child of Chance (It's absurd to say that truth . . .)

The Dear Liar (Sylvia Crest walked back to her . . .)

MG   *Strand Magazine*, Dec. 1921. The Dear Liar.

The Medieval Mind (There can be no question . . .)

MG   *Thriller*, 291, 1 Sept. 1934. The Medieval Mind.

The Looker & the Leaper (Foley, the smoke-room oracle . . .)

BK   *The Thief in the Night*, (Digit). The Looker & the Leaper.

The Christmas Princess (There were times when John Bennett . . .)

MG   *Windsor Magazine*, Vol. 59, Dec. 1923 to May 1924. The Christmas Princess.

The Treasure of the Kalahari (Romance may come . . .)

Indian Magic (When love comes barging into . . .)

MG   *Thriller*, 293, 15 Sept. 1934. Indian Magic.

Clever One, The (see B58)

B29 **Clue of the New Pin, The** (The establishment of Yeh Ling . . .)
Hodder & Stoughton 1923, 1962.
Hodder & Stoughton 9d. Yellow Jackets. No. 3 1942.

B30 **Clue of the Silver Key, The** (Alt. title: The Silver Key) (They were all in this business . . .)
Hodder & Stoughton 1930 (Oct.) 1942, 1961.
Hodder & Stoughton 9d. Yellow Jackets; Pan Books 115, 149.

B31 **Clue of the Twisted Candle, The** (The 4.15 from Victoria . . .)
George Newnes 1918, 1926 abridged 1928, 1932, 1934.
Newnes New Size Novels 1928; Pan Books 1954. C. Å. Ransom & Co. Paper Covered Edition.

MG *Grand Magazine*, Vol. 28/9, Jan. 1916 to Feb. 1917. The Clue of the Twisted Candle.

B32 **Coat of Arms, The** (Alt. title: The Arranways Mystery) (Officially they called the big . . .)
Hutchinson 1931; Arrow 1962.

Colossus, The (see **B83**).

B33 **Council of Justice, The** (It is not for you or me to judge . . .)
Ward Lock & Co. 1908; Digit 1963.
Ward Lock 6d. Copyright novels 227.

Counterfeiter, The (see **B58**)

Criminal at Large (see **B64**)

B34 **Crimson Circle, The** (It is a ponderable fact that ...)
Hodder & Stoughton Aug. 1922. 1941.
Hodder & Stoughton 9d. Yellow Jackets.
Pan Books 1950.

N *Daily Express*, 6 Dec. 1921 to 3 Feb. 1922. The Crimson Circle.

Croakers, The (see **B36**)

Crooks of Society (see **B11**)

Daffodil Murder, The (see **B35**)

B35 **Daffodil Mystery, The** (Alt. title: The Daffodil Murder) (I am afraid I don't understand you. . .)
Ward Lock & Co. 1920, 1931, 1932, 1954.

MG *Answers*, 1665–1676. 24 Apr. to 10 July 1920. The Daffodil Murder.

B36 **Dark Eyes of London, The** (Alt. title: The Croakers) (Larry Holt sat before the Café de ...)
Ward Lock & Co. 1924, 1932, 1954.

MG *Answers* 1718–1731, 30 Apr. to 30 July 1921. The Dark Eyes of London.

B37 **Daughters of the Night, The** (Jim Bartholomew, booted and spurred ...)
Newnes New Size Novels 1925; George Newnes 1928, 1928.
C. A. Ransom & Co. Paper covered edition.

MG *Grand Magazine*, Vol. 39, Mar. to Aug. 1921
The Daughters of the Night.

B38 **Day of Uniting, The** (By the sign of a printer's
steel table . . .)
Hodder & Stoughton 1926.
Hodder & Stoughton 9d. Yellow Jackets.

B39 **Debt Discharged, A** (On the afternoon of
March 4th 1913 . . .)
Ward Lock & Co. 1916; Digit 1963.

Destroying Angel, The (see **B7**)

B40 **Devil Man, The** (Alt. titles Sinister Street;
The Life & Death of Charles Peace; Silver
Steel) (On the western outskirts of Shef-
field . . .)
Collins 1931; Digit 1963.

Diamond Men, The (see **B48**)

Diana of Kara Kara (see **B43**)

B41 **Door with Seven Locks, The** (Dick Martin's
last official . . .)
Hodder & Stoughton 1926; Pan Books 1960.
Hodder & Stoughton 9d. Yellow Jackets.

MG *All Sports*, 300–313, 23 May to 29 Aug. 1925.
The Door with Seven Locks.

B42 **Double, The** (Alt. title: Sinister Halls) (When
Dick Staines left . . .)
Hodder & Stoughton Jan. 1928, Aug. 1953,
1958; Pan Books.

B43 **Double Dan** (Alt. title: Diana of Kara Kara)
(She is an orphan said Mr. Collings . . .)
Hodder & Stoughton Oct. 1924, 1937, 1954.
Hodder & Stoughton 9d. Yellow Jackets.

MG   *Happy Magazine*, 62–68, Jul. 1927 to Jan.
1928. Double Dan.

MG   *Grand Magazine*, vol. 45, Mar. to Aug. 1924.
Diana the Disturbing.

B44 **Down Under Donovan** (Curse the luck . . .)
Ward Lock & Co. 1918; Digit 1963.
Ward Lock 6d. Copyright novels 265.

B45 **Duke in the Suburbs, The** (The author who is
merely an inventor . . .)
Ward Lock & Co. 1909; Digit 1963.
Ward Lock 6d. Copyright novels 289.

Edgar Wallace: a short biography (see **B124**)

Edgar Wallace by Himself (see **B124**)

SS   **B46** **Educated Evans**
Webster Publications 1924; Collins 1929;
Tallis Press Ltd. 1967.

THE BROTHERHOOD (Inspector Pine was some-
thing more . . .)
MR. HOMASTER'S DAUGHTER (Mr. Homaster's
daughter was undoubtedly . . .)
THE COOP (Sometimes they referred to Mr.
Yardley . . .)
THE SNOUT (Saturday night in High Street,
Camden Town . . .)

Mr. Kirz buys a £5 Special (In an inner waistcoat pocket . . .)

Micky the Shopper (Educated Evans was sitting in . . .)

The Dreamer (It is a popular delusion . . .)

The Gift Horse (Men may acquire fame in a night . . .)

Straight from the Horse's Mouth (It is generally believed in . . .)

The Goods (It is an axiom that the . . .)

The Perfect Lady ('If', said Inspector Pine . . .)

The Proud Horse (Educated Evans left the Italian . . .)

Through the Card ('I have often wondered', said . . .)

Educated Man-Good Evans, The (see B68)

SS   **B47**   **Elegant Edward**

Readers Library 1928.

The Rum Runner (There is this about every man . . .)

Mr. Macmillan shares his Possessions (Elegant Edward not without reason . . .)

A Fortune in Tin (Elegant Edward dealt in a stable line . . .)

Papinico for the Scot (Mr. Edward Farthingdale . . .)

The Amateur Detective (A desire for vengeance . . .)

Double Bluff (You can well understand . . .)

THE MACK PUMP (The vulgarity of Senor Don
Alphonso . . .)

Eve's Island (see **B25**)
Allied Newspapers; Newnes New Size Novels
1926; Newnes 1927, 1928, 1928, 1935; Digit
Books 1961, 1962; C. A. Ransom & Co.
Paper covered edition.

Extra Girl, The (see **B8**)

B48 **Face in the Night, The** (Alt. titles: The
Diamond Men; The Ragged Princess) (The
fog which was later to descend . . .)
John Long 1924, 1926; Cherry Tree Books
No. 25 1938; Arrow 1961.
News of the World, 4209–4220, 29 June 1924
to 14 Sept. 1924. The Diamond Men.

B49 **Famous Scottish Regiments** (No country in
the world has a brigade . . .)
Our Fighting Forces No. 4 1914, George
Newnes.

B50 **Feathered Serpent, The** (Alt. titles: Inspector
Wade; Inspector Wade & the Feathered Ser-
pent) (What annoyed Peter Dewin most . . .)
Hodder & Stoughton Apr. 1927, Mar. 1951,
1952, 1958
Weekly Telegraph, 3370–3382, 20 Nov. 1926
to 12 Feb. 1927. The Feathered Serpent.

B51 **Fellowship of the Frog, The** (A dry radiator
coincided with a burst tyre . . .)

Ward Lock & Co. Jan. 1925; Digit 1963.
Ward Lock 6d. Copyright novels 241.

N   *People*, 23. Dec. 1923–6 Apr. 1924. The Fellowship.

NF   **B52**   **Fieldmarshal Sir John French** (When we are dealing with great men . . .)
George Newnes 1914.

SS   **B53**   **Fighting Scouts, The**
C. A. Pearson 1919.

     THE GENTLEMEN FROM INDIANA (Lieutenant Baxter was writing . . .)

MG   *Novel Magazine*, Oct. 1918. The Gentlemen from Indiana.

     THE DUKE'S MUSEUM (When the Grand Duke . . .)

MG   *Novel Magazine*, Nov. 1918. The Duke's Museum.

     THE KINDERGARTEN (The entry of the United States . . .)

MG   *Novel Magazine*, Dec. 1918. The Kindergarten.

     BOY BILLY BEST (Tam o' the Scouts sat . . .)
     THE WAGER OF RITTMEISTER VON HAARDEN (There is amongst the children . . .)

MG   *Novel Magazine*, Jan. 1919. The Wager of Rittmeister Von Haarden.

     THE DEBUT OF WILLIAM BEST (There is a loneliness . . .)

MG   *Novel Magazine*, Feb. 1919. The Debut of William Best.

     THE CLOUD FISHERS (Are you going . . .)

MG	*Novel Magazine*, Apr. 1919. The Cloud Fishers.

THE WOMAN IN THE STORY (Tam walked to the door . . .)

MG	*Novel Magazine*, Mar. 1919. The Woman in the Story.

THE INFANT SAMUEL (Tam said Billy . . .)

MG	*Novel Magazine*, May 1919. The Infant Samuel.

CSS	**B54**	**Fighting Snub Reilly**

George Newnes 1929.

All stories reprinted in Forty Eight Short Stories.

FIGHTING SNUB REILLY (Ten minutes before Snub Reilly . . .)

MG	*Strand Magazine*, Jan. 1922. Fighting Snub Reilly.

JIMMY'S BROTHER (I feel I should like to know . . .)

THE CHRISTMAS CUP (Colonel Desboro was an easy . . .)

MG	*E.W.M.M.* (Br.), No. 29, Dec. 1966. The Christmas Cup.
MG	*Royal Magazine*, 1929. He Who Could Ride.
MG	*Windsor Magazine*, Vol. 63, Dec. 1925 to May 1926. The Christmas Cup.
BK	*The Undisclosed Client*. The Christmas Cup.

THE MAN IN THE GOLF HUT (He walked down the stairs . . .)

MG	*Grand Magazine*, Vol. 37, Mar. to Aug. 1920. The Man in the Golf Hut.

A ROMANCE IN BROWN (Romance? Yes of a kind . . .)

MG   *Happy Magazine*, No. 8. Jan. 1923. A Romance in Brown.

A PERFECT GENTLEMAN (Mrs. Leverton Carn . . .)
KID GLOVE HARRY (Mr. Solomon Parsons . . .)
NIG-NOG (This story is about a matter . . .)

B55   **Flat 2** (A shot range out sharply . . .)
John Long 1927; Arrow 1961;

MG   Abridged version: *Ideas*, 1091–1095, 30 Jan. to 27 Feb. 1926. By Whose Hand.

MG   *Detective Magazine*, Nos. 1, 2, 3, 7, 1923. Flat 2.

B56   **Flying Fifty-Five, The** (Stella Barrington came through . . .)
Hutchinson 1922; Arrow 1961.

N   *News of the World*, 4090–4106, 19 Mar. to July 1922. The Flying Fifty-Five.

B57   **Flying Squad, The** (Ladys Stairs was a crazy wooden house . . .)

Hodder & Stoughton May 1928, 1951; Pan Books 1963;
Play: Hodder & Stoughton 1929.

B58   **Forger, The** (Alt. titles: The Clever One; The Counterfeiter) (The big consulting room at 903 . . .)

Hodder & Stoughton 1927, abr. 1938; Pan Books 1960.
Hodder & Stoughton 9d. Yellow Jackets.

CSS   **B59**   **For Information Received**
George Newnes 1929.

FOR INFORMATION RECEIVED (In the days of his youth . . .)

SNARES OF PARIS (Johnny Kelly, in the outward guise . . .)

A BUSINESS TRAINING (It was Winifred Laudermere . . .)

MG   *Pan*, Vol. 7, No. 10, April 1922. A Business Training.

MISS PRENTISS TELLS A LIE (It was a strange meeting . . .)

A PRIESTESS OF OSIRIS (Between Camden Town . . .)

MG   *Royal Magazine*, March 1923. Lure of Strange Gods.

THE TIMID ADMIRER (Mirabelle Stoll read the morning paper)

MG   *Grand Magazine*, Vol. 44, Sept. 1923 to Feb. 1924. The Timid Admirer.

THE JEWEL (This man said Dandy Lang . . .)
FINDINGS ARE KEEPINGS (Findings are keepings . . .)

BK   *Forty Eight Short Stories*. Findings are Keepings.

BK   *The Prison Breakers*. Findings are Keepings.
BK   *The Thief in the Night* (Digit). Findings are Keepings.

THE EAR OF THE SANCTUARY (When men in all sincerity . . .)

MG   *Royal Magazine*, Aug. 1922. The Ear of the Sanctuary.

CSS **B60** **Forty Eight Short Stories**
George Newnes 1929.

1. THE CAT BURGLAR (Old Tom Burkes used
to say . . .)

BK   (Digit). *The Terror*. The Cat Burglar.

1. THE PICK UP (It was the day before . . .)

MG   *John Bull Summer Annual*, 1927. The Pick Up.

1. DISCOVERING REX (In the office of the
Public Prosecutor . . .)
1. THE KNOW HOW (What you need Dian . . .)

1. WHITE STOCKING (John Trevor was not a
jealous man . . .)

MG   *Grand Magazine*, Vol. 41, March to Aug.
1922. White Stocking.

MG   *Thriller*, 312, 26 Jan. 1935. White Stocking.
N   *Evening Standard*, 6 June 1934. White Stocking.

1. THE CLUE OF MONDAYS SETTLING (It did
not seem possible . . .)

MG   *E.W.M.M.* (Br.), No. 8, Mar. 1965. The Clue
of Mondays Settling.

BK   *Fifty Masterpieces of Mystery*. The Clue of
Mondays Settling.

1. ESTABLISHING CHARLES BULLIVANT (There's
a new doctor . . .)

1. SENTIMENTAL SIMPSON (According to certain signs . . .)

MG   *E.W.M.M.* (Br.), No. 7, Feb. 1965. The Fall
of Sentimental Simpson.

MG   *Happy Magazine*, No. 1, June 1922. The
Sentimental Crook.

2. FIGHTING SNUB REILLY (Ten minutes
before Snub Reilly . . .)

MG   *Strand Magazine*, Jan. 1922. Fighting Snub Reilly.

2. JIMMY'S BROTHER (I feel I should like to know . . .)

2. THE CHRISTMAS CUP (Colonel Desboro was an easy . . .)

MG   *E.W.M.M.* (Br.), No. 29, Dec. 1966. The Christmas Cup.

MG   *Windsor Magazine*, Vol. 63, Dec. 1925 to May 1926. The Christmas Cup.

BK   *The Undisclosed Client*. The Christmas Cup.

MG   *Royal Magazine*, 1929. He Who Could Ride.

2. THE MAN IN THE GOLF HUT (He walked down the stairs. . .)

MG   *Grand Magazine*, Vol. 37, March to Aug. 1920. The Man in the Golf Hut.

2. A ROMANCE IN BROWN (Romance? Yes I suppose . . .)

MG   *Happy Magazine*, No. 8, Jan. 1923. A Romance in Brown.

2. A PERFECT GENTLEMAN (Mrs. Leverton Carn . . .)

2. KID GLOVE HARRY (Mr. Soloman Parsons . . .)

2. NIG-NOG (This is a story about a matter . . .)

3. THE PRISON BREAKERS (It was the sort of thing . . .)

MG   *E.W.M.M.* (Br.), No. 30, Jan. 1967. The Prison Breakers.

MG   *Thriller*, 288, 11 Aug. 1934. The Prison Breakers.

3. FINDINGS ARE KEEPINGS (Findings are keepings . . .)

BK	*The Thief in the Night* (Digit). Findings are keepings.
BK	*For Information Received.* Findings are Keepings.
	3. THE JEWEL BOX (There were very few moments when . . .)
	3. THE UNDISCLOSED CLIENT (A snowy night in early March . . .)
BK	*The Undisclosed Client.* The Undisclosed Client.
	3. VIA MADEIRA (This story concerns four people . . .)
BK	*The Thief in the Night* (Digit). Via Madeira.
	3. THE COMPLEAT CRIMINAL (Mr. Felix O'Hara Golbeater . . .)
MG	20 *Story Magazine*, Jan. 1930. The Perfect Criminal.
BK	*The Thief in the Night* (Digit). The Compleat Criminal.
	3. REDBEARD (One of the most jealously guarded secrets . . .)
	3. BULFOX ASLEEP (People say that Bulfox was a fool . . .)
MG	*Novel Magazine*, Apr. 1913. A Question of Honour.
MG	*Pearsons Weekly*, 1980, 7 July 1928. A Question of Honour.
MG	20 *Story Magazine*, Jan. 1931. Bulfox Asleep.
	4. THE LITTLE GREEN MAN (An understanding disturbed or terminated . . .)
BK	*The Undisclosed Client.* The Little Green Man.
	4. CODE No. 2 (The secret service never . . .)
MG	*Strand Magazine* Vol. ? Jan. to June 1916. Code No. 2.

MG   *E.W.M.M.* (Br.), No. 22, May 1966 Code. No. 2.

4. THE STRETELLI CASE (Detective Inspector John Mackenzie . . .)

MG   *Thriller*, 286, 28 July 1934. The Stretelli Case.

BK   *The Terror* (Digit). The Stretelli Case.

4. THE MAN WHO NEVER LOST (The man in the grey . . .)

MG   *Town Topics*, 383/4, 27 Dec. 1919 to 3 Jan. 1920. The Man Who Never Lost.

MG   *E.W.M.M.* (Br.), No. 11, June 1965. The Man Who Never Lost.

MG   *Thriller*, 290, 25 Aug. 1934. The Man Who Never Lost.

4. CHRISTMAS EVE AT THE CHINA DOG (Inventors are proverbially . . .)

4. CHUBB OF THE 'SLIPPER' (No doubt about Chubb's gift . . .)

MG   *Novel Magazine*, Oct. 1914. Chubb of the 'Slipper'.

4. THE KING'S BRAHM (There is a certain type of man . . .)

4. THE MAN WHO KILLED HIMSELF (Preston Somerville was standing . . .)

MG   *Royal Magazine*, Feb. 1920. The Man Who Killed Himself.

5. CIRCUMSTANTIAL EVIDENCE (Colonel Chartres Dane lingered . . .)

MG   *Strand Magazine*, Aug. 1922. Circumstantial Evidence.

BK   *Black Cap*. Circumstantial Evidence.

MG   *E.W.M.M.* (Br.), No. 9 Apr. 1965. Circumstantial Evidence.

5. THE CHILD OF CHANCE (It's absurd to say that truth . . .)

5. THE DEAR LIAR (Sylvia Crest walked back to her . . .)

MG *Strand Magazine*, Dec. 1921. The Dear Liar.

5 THE MEDIEVAL MIND (There can be no question . . .)

MG *Thriller*, 291, 1 Sept. 1934. The Medieval Mind.

5. THE LOOKER AND THE LEAPER (Foley, the smoke-room oracle . . .)

BK *The Thief in the Night* (Digit). The Looker & the Leaper.

5. THE CHRISTMAS PRINCESS (There were times when John Bennett . . .)

MG *Windsor Magazine*, Vol. 59, Dec. 1923 to May 1924. The Christmas Princess.

5. THE TREASURE OF THE KALAHARI (Romance may come . . .)

5. INDIAN MAGIC (When love comes barging into . . .)

MG *Thriller*, 293, 15 Sept. 1934. Indian Magic.

6. IN THRALL (Who knows where I may sleep tonight . . .)

MG *Saint Magazine*, (Br.), Jan. 1963. Christmas Bondage; also in *Grand Magazine*.

6. ON THE WITNEY ROAD (Tom Curtis said nothing . . .)

MG *Windsor Magazine*, Vol. 61, Dec. 1924 to May 1925. On the Witney Road.

6. MOTHER O'MINE (They called Ian Cranford . . .)

MG *Royal Magazine*, March 1920. Mother o' Mine.

6. THE GREEK POROPULOS (At Carolina, in the Transvaal . . .)

BK   *The Thief in the Night* (Digit). The Greek Poropulos.

MG   *E.W.M.M.* (Br.), No. 23, June 1966. The Killer of Lioski.

MG   *Weekly Tale Teller*, 81, 19 Nov. 1910. The Greek Poropulos.

6. THE GOVERNOR OF CHI-FOO (In Chi-Foo as in the forbidden . . .)

BK   *The Undisclosed Client*. The Governor of Chi-Foo.

6. A TRYST WITH GHOSTS (Once upon a time . . .)

6. THE WEAKLING (Rex Madlon was a nice boy . . .)

MG   *Pearsons Weekly*, 1949, 3 Dec. 1927. The Weakling.

6. JAKE'S BROTHER BILL (The effect of wine . . .)

MG   *Royal Magazine*, Apr. 1922. Jake's Brother Bill.

All stories were published in the following collections:
1. The Cat Burglar.
2. Fighting Snub Reilly.
3. The Prison Breakers.
4. The Little Green Man.
5. Circumstantial Evidence.
6. The Governor of Chi-Foo.

B61   **Four Just Men, The** (If you leave the Plaza del . . .)

Tallis Press 1905; George Newnes 1911, 1913; Newnes Trench Library 1919; Newnes 7d. Novels No. 41, 1921; Hodder & Stoughton 1926; Newnes New Size Novels 1926; George Newnes 1927, 1928; Penguin Books

No. 64: 1936; Pan Books 1950, 1953.
C. A. Ransom Paper backed edition.

B62 **Four Square Jane** (Alt. title: The Fourth Square) (Mr. Joe Lewinstein slouched to one . . .)
Readers Library 1929; New Chevron Series No. 101, 1940.
Digit 1961, 1962.

B63 **Fourth Plague, The** (South of Florence by some sixty miles . . .)
Ward Lock & Co. 1913; Digit 1963.
Ward Lock 6d. Copyright novels 257.

Fourth Square, The (see **B62**)

B64 **Frightened Lady, The** (Alt. titles: The Case of the Frightened Lady; The Mystery of the Frightened Lady; Criminal at Large) (American footmen aren't natural . . .)
Hodder & Stoughton 1932, 1949, 1956, 1964.
Hodder & Stoughton 9d. Yellow Jackets.
Play: (The Case of) 3 acts. French's acting Edition 1932, 1934.

Gallows Hand, The (see **B151**)

Gangsters Come to London, The (see **B168**)

Gaol-Breakers, The (see **B167**)

B65 **Gaunt Stranger, The** (Alt. titles: The Ringer; Police Work) This was not identical to The Ringer, see note under 'The Ringer'.

(Flanders Lane, Deptford, is narrow and dingy . . .)
Hodder & Stoughton 1925.

B66 **Ghost of Downhill, The**
Readers Library Apr. June, July, Sept. 1929, Mar. 1930.

THE GHOST OF DOWNHILL (It was of course a coincidence . . .)

MG   *E.W.M.M.* (Br.), No. 1, Aug. 1964. The Ghost of Downhill.

THE QUEEN OF SHEBA'S BELT (I suppose there's nothing more to be said. . .)

MG   *Grand Magazine*, Vol. 21, Mar. to June 1914. The Queen of Sheba's Belt.

MG   *E.W.M.M.* (Br.), No. 4, Nov. 1964. The Queen of Sheba's Belt.

Girl from Scotland Yard, The (see B144)

B67 **Golden Hades, The** (Alt. title: Stamped in Gold) (Frank Alwin lifted his manacled hands . . .)
Collins Oct. 1929; Detective Story Club, London & Glasgow 1933; Hodder & Stoughton 1962; Pan Books 1966.

Revised story from: *Ideas* 765 to 770, 5 Nov. 1919 to 10 Dec. 1919. Branded Millions.

SS   **B68** **Good Evans** (Alt. title: The Educated Man—Good Evans)
Websters Publications 1927; Collins 1930; Tallis Press 1967.

A CHANGE OF PLAN (It was when an excited . . .)

MR. EVANS DOES A BIT OF GAS WORK (Mr. Siniter was wider than . . .)

EDUCATION AND COMBINATIONS (Mr. Evans had concluded . . .)

THE OTHER LUBESES (Educated Evans being by nature . . .)

MR. EVANS PULLS OFF A REAL COOP (The Miller regarded his . . .)

THE NICE-MINDED GIRL (There is no doubt at all . . .)

THE MUSICAL TIP (It is a curious fact that . . .

PSYCHOLOGY AND THE TIPSTER (Mr. Lube had a cousin . . .)

THE SHOWING UP OF EDUCATED EVANS (It was unfortunate that Mr. Yevers . . .)

THE SUBCONSCIOUS MIND (The eternal quest for information . . .)

MR. EVANS HAS A WELL SCREWED HEAD (As the field came round . . .)

THE TWISTING OF ARTHUR COLLEYBORN (One of the hardest things . . .)

THE KIDNAPPING OF MR. EVANS (There was a certain head lad . . .)

EDUCATED EVANS DECLARES TO WIN (Mr. Evans had many detractors . . .)

FOR EVANS' SAKE (Detective Inspector Challoner strolled along . . .)

THE PARTICULAR BEAUTY (Educated Evans had many promising . . .)

THE LAST COOP OF ALL (He's a rum looking devil . . .)

CSS **B69** **Governor of Chi-Foo, The**
George Newnes 1929.
All stories reprinted in Forty Eight Short Stories.

THE GOVERNOR OF CHI-FOO (In Chi-Foo as in the forbidden . . .)

BK
The Undisclosed Client. The Governor of Chi-Foo.

IN THRALL ('Who knows where I may sleep tonight . . .')

MG
Saint Magazine (Br.), Jan. 1963. Christmas Bondage; also in *Grand Magazine*.

ON THE WITNEY ROAD (Tom Curtis said nothing . . .)

MG
Windsor Magazine, Vol. 61, Dec. 1924 to May 1925. On the Witney Road.

MOTHER O'MINE (They called Ian Cranford . . .)

MG
Royal Magazine, March 1920. Mother o'Mine

JAKE'S BROTHER BILL (The effect of wine . . .)

MG
ROYAL MAGAZINE, April 1922. Jake's Brother Bill.

THE WEAKLING (Rex Madlon was a nice boy . . .)

MG
Pearsons Weekly, 1942, 3 Dec. 1927. The Weakling.

A TRYST WITH GHOSTS (Once upon a time . . .)

THE GREEK POROPULOS (At Carolina, in the Transvaal . . .)

MG
E.W.M.M. (Br.), No. 23, June 1966. The Killer of Lioski.

MG
Weekly Tale Teller, 81, 19 Nov. 1910. The Greek Poropulos.

BK *The Thief in the Night* (Digit). The Greek Poropulos.

B70 Green Archer, The (Spike Holland scrawled his last word . . .)
Hodder & Stoughton 1923, Nov. 1928, 1950, 1953.

MG *Detective Magazine*, 18–31, 20 July 1923 to Jan. 1924. The Green Archer.

B71 Green Pack, The (novel of the play) by Robert Curtis) (Mount Lodge, Kensington, bore every . . .)
Hutchinson Oct. 1933.

Play in 3 acts by Edgar Wallace, London/ N.Y. 1933.
Scene: Da Silvas Hotel, Lobito Bay.
Mark: 'What's that tune Tubby . . .'

B72 Green Ribbon, The (Walking up Lower Regent Street . . .)
Hutchinson 1929; Arrow Books 1953, 1957, 1962.

N *News of the World*, 4479–4489, 1 Sept. to 10 Nov. 1929. The Green Ribbon.

B73 Green Rust, The (I don't know whether there's a law . . .)
Ward Lock & Co. 1919, 1934, 1956; Digit 1963.

N *News of the World*, 3918–3933. The Green Terror.

B74 **Grey Timothy** (Alt. title: Pallard the Punter)
(Brian Pallard wrote to his uncle . . .)
Ward Lock & Co. 1913; Digit 1963.
Ward Lock 6d. Copyright novels 201.

Gunman's Bluff (see **B75**)

B75 **Gunner, The** (Alt. titles: Children of the Poor;
Gunman's Bluff) (But are you going to marry
him . . .)
John Long 1928; Collins 1933; Arrow Books
1953, 1960, 1963.

LSS **B76** **Guv'nor & Other Stories, The**
Collins 1932.

THE GUV'NOR (The affair of Mary Keen . . .)
THE MAN WHO PASSED (Mr. Mannering was
called 'the Captain' . . .)

MG   *Thriller*, 105, 7 Feb. 1931. The Man from
Sing Sing.

THE TREASURE HOUSE (Mr. J. G. Reeder did
odd things . . .)

BK   *Mr. J. G. Reeder Returns:* The Treasure
House.

MG   *Thriller*, 106, 14 Feb. 1931. The Prisoner of
Seven Ways.

THE SHADOW MAN (When Mr. Reeder went to
New York . . .)

BK   *Mr. J. G. Reeder Returns:* The Shadow Man.
MG   *Thriller*, 156, 30 Jan. 1932. The Shadow Man.

LSS **B77** **Guv'nor, The** (also in **B76**)
Collins 1932; Hodder & Stoughton revised
1965.

81

D

THE GUV'NOR (The affair of Mary Keen . . .)
THE MAN WHO PASSED (Mr. Mannering was called 'the Captain' . . .)

MG   *Thriller*, 105, 7 Feb. 1931. The Man from Sing Sing.

Hairy Arm, The (see **B98**)

B78   **Hand of Power, The** (Alt. title: The Proud Sons of Ragusa) (A gale of wind and rain swept . . .)
John Long 1927; Arrow Books.

NF   **B79**   **Heroes All: Gallant Deeds of the War** (Let me start this volume . . .)
George Newnes 1914.

His Devoted Squealer (see **B98**)

B80   **India Rubber Men, The** (Alt. titles: Wolves of the Waterfront; The Pool) (In the murk of a foggy morning . . .)
Hodder & Stoughton 1929; Pan Books 1952, 1956.
Hodder & Stoughton 9d. Yellow Jackets.

MG   *Pearsons Weekly*, 1994–2014, 13 Oct. 1928 to 2 Mar. 1929. The India-Rubber Men.

Inspector Wade (see **B50**)

Inspector Wade and the Feathered Serpent (see **B50**)

SS   **B81**   **Iron Grip, The** (Alt. title: Wireless Bryce)
Readers Library 1930; New Chevron Series

No. 88, 1941. Allied Newspapers in conjunction with Readers Library.

THE MAN FROM 'DOWN UNDER' (Captain Jack Bryce, inscribed in . . .)

THE WILFUL MISS COLEBROOK (Well, Captain Bryce, I didn't . . .)

THE TYRANT OF THE HOUSE (Jack Bryce was taking a little . . .)

THE KIDNAPPED TYPIST (Jack Bryce surveyed the world from . . .)

THE VLAKFONTAIN DIAMOND (It was ten o'clock on a foggy . . .)

A QUESTION OF HOURS (There are skeletons in a great . . .)

THE STRANGE CASE OF ANITE BRADE (No man realised more . . .)

THE DISAPPEARING LADY ('Jack', said Hemmer one morning . . .)

THE CASE OF AN HEIRESS (Much of Messrs Hemmer & Hemmer's . . .)

THE BEAUTIFUL MISS M'GREGGOR (Captain Jack Bryce was not particularly . . .)

Island of Galloping Gold, The (see **B25**)
Newnes Copyright Novels 421; Newnes 1916; Newnes 7d. Novels, No. 11, 1920.

B82 **Jack o'Judgment** (They picked up the young man called 'Snow' . . .)
Ward Lock & Co. 1920; Digit 1963.
Ward Lock 6d. Copyright novels 206.

MG   *Boys Favourite*, 1–11, 4 May to 13 July 1929. Jack o'Judgment.

N   *Daily Express*, 7 Oct. to 22 Nov. 1919. Jack o'Judgment.

B83 **Joker, The** (Alt. titles: The Colossus; The Park Lane Mystery) (Mr. Stratford Harlow was a gentleman . . .)
Hodder & Stoughton 1926; Hodder & Stoughton 9d. Yellow Jackets; Pan Books 1950, 1951, 1954, 1960.

B84 **Just Men of Cordova, The** (The man who sat at the marble-topped . . .)
Ward Lock & Co. 1917, 1954; Digit 1963.
Ward Lock 6d. Copyright novels 235.

B85 **Kate Plus Ten** ('Strategy', growled the General . . .)
Ward Lock & Co. 1919, 1928; Digit 1963.
Ward Lock 6d. Copyright novels 261.

SS   **B86** **Keepers of the King's Peace, The**
Ward Lock & Co. 1917; Digit May 1963.

BONES, SANDERS & ANOTHER (To Isongo, which stands . . .)

MG   *Weekly Tale Teller*, 357, 4 Mar. 1916. Bones, Sanders & Another.

BONES CHANGES HIS RELIGION (Captain Hamilton of the King's Houssas . . .)

MG   *Windsor Magazine*, Vol. 44, June to Nov. 1916. The Branding of Bones.

THE MAKER OF STORMS (Everybody knows that water drawn . . .)

MG
    Windsor Magazine, Vol. 44, June to Nov. 1916. The Maker of Storms.

BONES AND THE WIRELESS (Ko-Boru, the headman of Bingini . . .)

MG
    Windsor Magazine, Vol. 44, June to Nov. 1916. Bones & the Wireless.

THE REMEDY (Beyond the far hills which no no man . . .)

MG
    Windsor Magazine, Vol. 44, June to Nov. 1916. The Remedy.

THE MEDICINE MAN (At the flood season before the . . .)

MG
    Windsor Magazine, Vol. 44, June to Nov. 1916. The Medicine Man.

BONES, KING-MAKER (Patricia Hamilton, an observant . . .)

MG
    Windsor Magazine, Vol. 45, Dec. 1916 to May 1917. Bones, King-Maker.

THE TAMER OF BEASTS (Native folk at any rate . . .)

MG
    Windsor Magazine, Vol. 45, Dec. 1916 to May 1917. The Tamer of Beasts.

THE MERCENARIES (There was a large brown desk . . .)

MG
    Windsor Magazine, Vol. 45, Dec. 1916 to May 1917. The Mercenaries.

THE WATERS OF MADNESS (Unexpected things happen . . .)

MG
    Windsor Magazine, Vol. 45, Dec. 1916 to May 1917. The Waters of Madness.

EYE TO EYE (Bones, said Captain Hamilton . . .)

MG
    Windsor Magazine, Vol. 45, Dec. 1916 to May 1917. Eye to Eye.

THE HOODED KING (There was a certain Portugese . . .)

MG   *Windsor Magazine*, Vol. 46, June to Nov. 1917. The Hooded King.

CSS **B87** **Killer Kay**
George Newnes. No date, believed 1930.

KILLER KAY (When the Eastbourne Express . . .)

THE BUSINESS WOMAN (Certain features of the . . .)

BLUE SUIT (Many men had tried to . . .)

BATTLE LEVEL (Dalberry came down the . . .)

THE AIR TAXI (Beneath them was a dull . . .)

MG   *Grand Magazine*, Vol. 40, Sept. 1921 to Feb. 1922. Tam's Air-Taxi.

THE CONVENIENT SEA (There were times when . . .)

THE VAMP & THE LIBRARIAN (Some clever people can . . .)

THIEVES MAKE THIEVES (If you had told Miss Cayling . . .)

MG   *E.W.M.M.* (Br.), No. 2, Sept. 1964. Thieves Make Thieves.

    B88 **King by Night, A** (Dr Arnold Eversham sat at his broad . . .)
John Long 1925, 1926; Leasure Library; Universal Library 1930; Cherry Tree Books No. 38, 1939; Arrow 1954, 1957, 1961.

MG   *Boys' Favourite*, 20–33, 14 Sept. to 14 Dec. 1929. A King by Night.

NF **B89** **Kitchener's Army & the Territorial Forces**.
(Kitchener's Army! a phrase which may well
stand . . .)
George Newnes 1915; 6 parts.

CSS **B90** **Lady Called Nita, The**
George Newnes; No date, believed 1930.

THE LADY CALLED NITA (The lady, called by
her . . .)

THE MAN WHO MARRIED HIS COOK (One
afternoon in May . . .)
MG *Royal Magazine*, Feb. 1921. The Man Who
Married His Cook.

MR. SIGEE'S RELATIONS (Mr. Albert Sigee's
attitude . . .)
BK (Rewritten in Undisclosed Client—Change)
MG *E.W.M.M.* (Br.), No. 15, Oct. 1965. Duo in
Blue.
MG *Ideas*, 209, 17 Mar. 1909. Change.

THE KNIGHT WHO COULD NOT KNEEL (Daniel
Gree was grey . . .)

HER FATHER'S DAUGHTER (In the old days,
the Howarths . . .)
MG *Nash's Illustrated Weekly*, 19, 17 Jan. 1920. A
Girl Among Thieves.
MG 20 *Story Magazine*, Oct. 1929. Her Father's
Daughter.

THE DRAMATIC BUTLER (When Barbara Long
called . . .)
DIANA HELPS (Jack Saverley had serious . . .)
CON-LACTO IS STRENGTH (Between the Ken-
tish coast . . .)

B91 **Lady of Ascot, The** (Curiosity being one of the besetting sins . . .)
Hutchinson 1930; Arrow 1962.

CSS **B92** **Lady of Little Hell, The**
George Newnes 1929.

THE LADY OF LITTLE HELL (A dozen boisterous voices . . .)
THE GIRL FROM ETHER (Captain Race said . . .)
FATE & MR. HOKE (Lord Derrymere read the paragraph . . .)

MG *Grand Magazine*, Vol. 46, Sept. 1924 to Feb. 1925 A Deed of Gift.

DECLARED TO WIN (John Petworth came out of the army . . .)

MG *Grand Magazine*, Vol. 49, March to Aug. 1926. Declared to Win.

THE CROSS OF THE THIEF (Pamela Wilson once lectured . . .)

MG *Royal Magazine*, Sept. 1922. One with Authority.

BILL AND THE TOPPER (There was a very clever detective . . .)

MG *Pearsons Weekly*, 1942, 5 Oct. 1927. Bill & the Topper.

THE PRAYING GIRL (The girl drove into the Bahnhof . . .)

MG *Weekly Tale Teller*, 337, 16 Oct. 1915. The Praying Girl.

THE CUSTODY OF THE CHILD (There were times when Mrs. Harvey . . .)

MG *Pearsons Weekly*, 2054, 7 Dec. 1929. The Custody of the Child.

CSS	B93	**Last Adventure, The** Hutchinson 1934

LSS   BIG LITTLE BROTHER (John Calthorpe . . .)

THE LAST ADVENTURE (Most people who draw for a straight . . .)

THE TALKATIVE BURGLAR (The Duke smelt danger . . .)

MG   *Pearsons Weekly*, 1957, 28 Jan. 1928. The Talkative Burglar.

MG   *Novel Magazine*, Dec. 1912. The Talkative Burglar.

THE WILL & THE WAY (People only make such wills . . .)

MG   *Merry Magazine*, No. 13, July 1925. The Will and the Wont.

A JUDGE OF HORSES (There was a young man . . .)

THE PEDLAR IN THE MASK (Arthur Confort was a young man . . .)

MG   *Grand Magazine*, Vol. 40, Sept. 1921 to Feb. 1922. The Pedlar in the Mask.

MR JIGGS MAKES GOOD (Mr. Denny, of Lansfield . . .)

MG   *New Royal Magazine*, No. 1, Dec. 1930. Mr. Jiggs Makes Good.

THE TRIMMING OF SAM (Somebody saw Long Sam . . .)

MG   *Happy Magazine*, No. 12, May 1923. A Man of His Word.

THE WINNING TICKET (From her point of observation . . .)

MG   *Strand Magazine*, 1932. The Winning Ticket.

HIS GAME (The ninth guards were at dinner . . .)

MG   *Windsor Magazine*, Vol. 32, June to Nov. 1910. His Game.

THE DEVIL DOCTOR (George Rewen had a weakness . . .)

MG   *E.W.M.M.* (Br.), No. 28, Nov. 1966. The Devil Doctor.

THE ORIGINAL MRS. BLANEY (Mr. Michaloff Poginski . . .)

SS   **B94**   **Law of the Four Just Men, The** (A. Again the Three Just Men)
Hodder & Stoughton 1921, 1938, 1952.
Hodder & Stoughton 9d. Yellow Jackets.

THE MAN WHO LIVED AT CLAPHAM (The jury cannot accept . . .)

MG   *Strand Magazine*, May 1921. The Man Who Lived at Clampham.

THE MAN WITH THE CANINE TEETH (Murder my dear Manfred . . .)

MG   *Saint Magazine* (Br.), Oct. 1963. The Man with the Canine Teeth.

MG   *Strand Magazine*, June 1921. The Man with the Canine Teeth.

THE MAN WHO HATED EARTHWORMS (The death has occurred at Staines . . .)

MG   *Strand Magazine*, July 1921. The Man Who Hated Earthworms.

THE MAN WHO DIED TWICE (The interval between Acts II and III . . .)

MG   *Saint Magazine* (Br.), Apr. 1965. The Man Who Died Twice.

MG   *Strand Magazine*, Aug. 1921. The Man Who Died Twice.

THE MAN WHO HATED AMELIA JONES (There was a letter that came . . .)

MG   *Saint Magazine* (Br.), March 1963. The Man Who Hated Amelia Jones.

MG   *Strand Magazine*, Sept. 1921. The Man Who Hated Amelia Jones.

THE MAN WHO WAS HAPPY (On a pleasant evening . . .)

MG   *Strand Magazine*, Oct. 1921. The Man Who Was Happy.

THE MAN WHO LOVED MUSIC (The most striking characteristics . . .)

MG   *Thriller*, 319, 16 Mar. 1935. The Man Who Loved Music.

MG   *Novel Magazine*, Sept. 1921. The Man Who Loved Music.

THE MAN WHO WAS PLUCKED (On Sunday night Marlans Club . . .)

MG   *Thriller*, 325, 27 Apr. 1935. The Man Was Plucked.

THE MAN WHO WOULD NOT SPEAK (But for the fact that he was . . .)

MG   *Thriller*, 321, 30 Mar. 1935. The Man Who Would Not Speak.

MG   *Novel Magazine*, Aug. 1921. The Man Who Would Not Speak.

THE MAN WHO WAS ACQUITTED ('Have you noticed' said Leon Gonsalez . . .)

MG   *Thriller*, 335, 6 July 1935. The Man Who Was Acquitted.

A   **Law of the Three Just Men, The** (see **B5**)

SS   **B95**   **Lieutenant Bones**
Ward Lock & Co. 1918, 1952; Digit 1963.

LIEUTENANT BONES R.N. (There was a lawless . . .)

MG   *Windsor Magazine*, Vol. 46, June to Nov. 1917. Lieutenant Bones R.N.

THE SLEUTH (Mr. Commissioner Sanders sat in the . . .)

MG   *Windsor Magazine*, Vol. 46, June to Nov. 1917. The Sleuth.

A CHANGE OF MINISTRY (Lieutenant Augustus Tibbetts of the . . .)

MG   *Windsor Magazine*, Vol. 46, June to Nov. 1917. A Change of Ministry.

THE LOVER OF SANDERS (Ali Abid was a stoutish man . . .)

MG   *Windsor Magazine*, Vol. 46, June to Nov. 1917. The Lover of Sanders.

THE BREAKING POINT (Twice in the year of crops . . .)

MG   *Windsor Magazine*, Vol. 47, Dec. 1917 to May 1918. The Breaking Point.

THE MADNESS OF VALENTINE (Miss Valentine Decarron was . . .)

MG   *Windsor Magazine*, Vol. 47, Dec. 1917 to May 1918. The Madness of Valentine.

THE LEGENDEER ('Bones', said Captain Hamilton shaking . . .)

MG   *Windsor Magazine*, Vol. 47, Dec. 1917 to May 1918. The Legendeer.

THE FETISH STICK (Viewed from the sea . . .)

MG   *Windsor Magazine*, Vol. 47, Dec. 1917 to May 1918. The Fetish Stick.

THE PACIFIST (There's something about me . . .)

MG   *Windsor Magazine*, Vol. 47, Dec. 1917 to May 1918. The Pacifist.

THE SON OF SANDI (When Tigibini the headman . . .)

MG   *Windsor Magazine*, Vol. 47, Dec. 1917 to May 1918. The Son of Sandi.

KING ANDREAS (There were four generations . . .)

MG   *Windsor Magazine*, Vol. 48, June to Nov. 1918. King Andreas.

BONES & A LADY (Years ago before any . . .)

MG   *Windsor Magazine*, Vol. 46, June to Nov. 1917. Bones & a Lady.

THE LITTLE PEOPLE (In a country where gossip . . .)

MG   *Windsor Magazine*, Vol. 48. June to Nov. 1918. The Little People.

THE NORTHERN MEN (Patricia Hamilton awaited Bones . . .)

MG   *Windsor Magazine*, Vol. 48, June to Nov. 1918. The Northern Men.

Life & Death of Charles Peace, The (see **B40**)

CSS   **B96**   **Little Green Man, The**
George Newnes 1929.
All stories reprinted in Forty Eight Short Stories.

THE LITTLE GREEN MAN (An understanding disturbed or terminated . . .)

BK   *The Undisclosed Client:* The Little Green Man.
CODE NO. 2 (The secret service never . . .)

MG   *E.W.M.M.* (Br.), No. 22, May 1966. Code No. 2.

MG   *Strand Magazine*, Vol. ?, Jan to June 1916. Code No. 2.

THE STRETELLI CASE (Detective Inspector John Mackenzie . . .)

MG   *Thriller*, 286, 28 July 1934. The Stretelli Case.

BK   (Digit.) *The Terror:* The Stretelli Case.

THE MAN WHO NEVER LOST (The man in the grey . . .)

MG   *E.W.M.M.* (Br.), No. 11, June 1965. The Man Who Never Lost.

MG   *Thriller*, 290, 25 Aug. 1934. The Man Who Never Lost.

MG   *Town Topics*, 383/4, 21 Dec. 1919 to 3 Jan. 1920. The Man Who Never Lost.

CHRISTMAS EVE AT THE CHINA DOG (Inventors are proverbially . . .)

CHUBB OF THE 'SLIPPER' (No doubt about Chubb's gift . . .)

MG   *Novel Magazine*, Oct. 1914, Chubb of the 'Slipper'.

THE KING'S BRAHM (There is a certain type of man . . .)

THE MAN WHO KILLED HIMSELF (Preston Somerville was standing . . .)

MG   *Royal Magazine*, Feb. 1920. The Man Who Killed Himself.

SS   **B97**   **Lone House Mystery, The**
Collins 1929; Digit 1961, 1962.
Featuring Superintendant Minter.

THE LONE HOUSE MYSTERY (I am taking no credit out of . . .)

THE SOOPER SPEAKING (When people get short on topics . . .)

CLUES (I've got a smart alec of a . . .)

ROMANCE IN IT (Spending money said the Superintendent . . .)

B98 **Man at the Carlton, The** (Alt. titles: His Devoted Squealer; The Mystery of Mary Grier) (There was a man named Harry Stone . . .)
Hodder & Stoughton 1931; Pan Books 1963, 1964.
Hodder & Stoughton 9d. Yellow Jackets.
Daily Express, 16 Mar. to 21 Apr. 1931. The Man at the Carlton.

B99 **Man from Morocco, The** (U.S.A.: The Black; Alt. title: Souls in Shadows) (James Lexington Mortlake gentleman of leisure . . .)
John Long Jan. 1926; Cherry Tree Books No. 33 1938. Arrow Books 1961.
Answers, 1847, 20 Oct. 1923 to 1866, 1 Mar. 1924. Souls in Shadows (abridged).

B100 **Man Who bought London, The** (Night had come to the West End . . .)
Ward Lock & Co. 1915; Digit 1963.
Ward Lock 6d. Copyright novels 313.

B101 **Man Who Changed his Name, The** (Novel of the play by Robert Curtis) (Nita Clive was sitting in a deckchair . . .   )
Hutchinson Feb. 1935; Crime Book Society

N

MG

(Hutchinson). Play by Edgar Wallace 1929 ('Sunningbourne Lodge', Ascot . . .)

B102 Man Who Knew, The (The room was a small one . . .) George Newnes 1919, 1928, 1935; Newnes New Size Novels 1926; Newnes Copyright Novels 424; Panther Books No. 1217 1961. C. A. Ransom & Co. Paper-backed edition.

B103 Man Who Was Nobody, The (Well, you've got him! . . .)
Ward Lock & Co. 1927, 1956.

MG *Yes or No* (Gleaned by advertisement).

B104 Melody of Death, The (On the night of May 27th 1911 . . .)
J. Arrowsmith/Simpkin Marshall 1915, The Readers' Library, 1928; Allied Newspapers in conjunction with Readers Lib; New Chevron Series No. 68 1939, 1940; Macdonald (Date unknown).

B105 Million Dollar Story, The (John Sands had infinite faith in his star . . .)
George Newnes 1928, 1928, 1935; Newnes New Size Novels 1926; C. A. Ransom & Co. Paper covered edition.

MG *Novel Magazine*. The Woman with the Red Hands.

SS **B106 Mind of Mr. J. G. Reeder, The** (Alt. title: The Murder Book of Mr. J. G. Reeder.)
Hodder & Stoughton Sept. 1925, Sept. 1941;

Hodder & Stoughton 9d. Yellow Jackets;
Pan Books 1962.

THE POETICAL POLICEMAN (The day Mr.
Reeder arrived ...)

MG   *Thriller*, 304, 1 Dec. 1934. The Poet Policeman.

MG   *Saint Magazine* (Br.), Sept. 1955. The
Poetical Policeman.

MG   *Grand Magazine*, Vol. 46, Sept. 1924 to Feb.
1925. The Strange Case of the Night Watchman.

BK   *Fifty Famous Detectives in Fiction*: The
Poetical Policeman.

THE TREASURE HUNT (There is a tradition in
criminal ...)

MG   *Thriller*, 287, 4 Aug. 1934. The Treasure Hunt.

MG   *Saint Magazine* (Br.), Jan. 1956. The Treasure
of Mr. Reeder.

MG   *Grand Magazine*, Vol. 46, Sept. 1924 to Feb.
1925. The Treasure Hunt.

THE TROUPE (There was a quietude and
sedateness ...)

MG   *Thriller*, 307, 22 Dec. 1934. The Remarkable
Mr. Reeder.

MG   *E.W.M.M.* (Br.) No. 16, Nov. 1965. The
Remarkable Mr. Reeder.

MG   *Grand Magazine*, Vol. 46, Sept. 1924 to
Feb. 1925. A Place on The River.

THE STEALER OF MARBLE (Margaret Belman's
chiefest claim ...)

N   *Evening Standard*, 3 Aug. 1936. The Stealer of
Marble.

MG   *Grand Magazine*, Vol. 46, Sept. 1924 to Feb.
1925. The Telephone Box.

SHEER MELODRAMA (It was Mr. Reeder who planned . . .)

MG   *Thriller*, 289, 18 Aug. 1934. Sheer Melodrama.

MG   *E.W.M.M.* (Br.), No. 27, Oct. 1966. Sheer Melodrama.

MG   *Grand Magazine*, Vol. 47, Mar. to Aug. 1925. The Man from the East.

THE GREEN MAMBA (The spirit of exploration . . .)

MG   *Thriller*, 292, 8 Sept. 1934. The Green Mamba.

MG   *Grand Magazine*, Vol. 47, Mar. to Aug. 1925. The Dangerous Reptile.

THE STRANGE CASE (In the days of Mr. Reeder's youth . . .)

MG   *Grand Magazine*, Vol. 47, Mar. to Aug. 1925. The Weak Spot.

THE INVESTORS (There are seven million people . . .)

MG   *Thriller*, 294, 22 Sept. 1934. The Investors.

MG   *E.W.M.M.* (Br.), No. 25, Aug. 1966. They Walked Away.

MG   *Saint Magazine* (Br.), Aug. 1956. The Disappearing Investors.

MG   *Grand Magazine*, Vol. 47, Mar. to Aug. 1925. The Investors.

B107 Missing Million, The (You've dropped a flower, sir . . .)
John Long 1923, 1924; Leisure Library; Cherry Tree Books No. 48, 1939; Arrow Books 1961.

V   **B108 Mission that Failed, The**
T. Maskew Miller, South Africa 1898; little more than a pamphlet.

THE MISSION THAT FAILED.

THE PRAYER.

THE LAND OF THE NORTH.

SOME ADVENTURES OF JAMES JAWKINS ESQ.

JAMES GETS A BILLET.

A CRISIS.

AN IMPRESSION OF JAMES.

JAMES ON THE DEVELOPMENT OF THE
CAPETONIAN.

JAMES ON POLITICS.

THE GREATER GOD.

THE SONG OF THE ROODEDAM.

UNDER WHICH FLAG.

THE PATRIOTIC COLONIST.

THE SQUIRE.

THE SEA-NATION.

THE SONG OF THE BOUNDER.

THE GIDDY LITTLE MICROBE.

THE NUMBER ONE.

BRITANNIA TO HER FIRST BORN.

A TOMMY'S WELCOME.

GINGER JAMES.

THE DEPARTURE OF JAMES.

CSS   B109   **Mrs. William Jones & Bill**
              George Newnes. No date, believed 1930.

              MRS. WILLIAM JONES & BILL (Her eyes were
              sleepy eyes . . .)
MG   20 *Story Magazine*, Oct. 1922. Bill Jones &
              Mrs William Jones.

THE ADVENTURES OF GEORGE (George Gregory Sanworth was regarded . . .)

MG   *Windsor Magazine*, Vol. 33, Dec. 1910 to May 1911. The Adventures of George.

ACCORDING TO FREUD (The real seven ages of man's . . .)

Note: This is a rewritten version of 'The Clue of Monday's Settling', see: THE CAT BURGLAR. BONDAGE (The first waking hours of . . .); THE SOCIETY OF BRIGHT YOUNG PEOPLE (A man who calls his unprotected . . .)

MG   *Merry Magazine*, No. 8, Feb. 1925. The Fearful Four.

THE KING & THE EDITOR (The King read the letter again . . .)

CHRISTMAS PRESENTS (Lew Withersyne's 'magnificent car . . .)

Mr. Commissioner Sanders (see **B134**)

LSS   **B110** **Mr. J. G. Reeder Returns**

Collins 1934; Hoddei & Stoughton 1965 (revised)

THE TREASURE HOUSE (Mr. J. G. Reeder did odd things . . .)

BK   *The Guv'nor & Other Stories:* The Treasure House.

MG   *Thriller*, 106, 14 Mar. 1931. The Prisoner of Seven Ways.

THE SHADOW MAN (When Mr. Reeder went to New York . . .)

MG   *Thriller*, 156, 30 Jan. 1932. The Shadow Man.

BK   *The Guv'nor & Other Stories:* The Shadow Man.

B111 Mr. Justice Maxell (Alt. title: Take-a-chance Anderson) (It was two hours after the . . .) Ward Lock & Co. 1922, 1954; Digit 1963; Ward Lock 6d. Copyright novels 216.

A **Mr. Reeder Returns** (see **B76**)

SS **B112 Mixer, The**
Leisure Library; John Long 1927; Arrow 1962; John Long revised Apr. 1966; Cherry Tree Books No. 29 1938.

THE OUTWITTING OF PONY NELSON (Pony Nelson had clicked . . .)

MG *Topical Times*, 511, 31 Aug. 1929. The Outwitting of Pony Nelson.

THE GREAT GENEVA SWEEPSTAKE (Graeside is a very . . .)

MG *Topical Times*, 512, 7 Sept. 1929. The Great Geneva Sweepstake.

A SPECULATION IN SHARES (In one of the most fashionable . . .

MG *Topical Times*, 513, 14 Sept. 1929. A Speculation in Shares.

THE BANK THAT DID NOT FAIL (The Mixer walked aimlessly . . .)

MG *Topical Times*, 514, 21 Sept. 1929. The Bank that did not Fail.

MR LIMMERBURG'S WATERLOO ('Good' said Anthony . . .

MG *Topical Times*, 515, 28 Sept. 1929. **Mr.** Limmerburg's Waterloo.

A CLOSE CALL & ITS SEQUEL (Miss Millicent K. Yonker was a . . .)

MG   *Topical Times*, 517, 12 Oct. 1929. A Close Call & its Sequel.

How a Famous Master Criminal was Trapped (The residence of Mr. Heimer . . .)

MG   *Topical Times*, 516, 5 Oct. 1929. How a Famous Master Criminal was Trapped.

Mr. Sparkes, the Detective (Do you remember Millicent K. Yonker . . .)

MG   *Topical Times*, 518, 19 Oct. 1929. Mr. Sparkes, the Detective.

The Submarine-Chaser Coup (There's one thing that worries . . .

MG   *Topical Times*, 519, 28 Oct. 1929. The Submarine-Chaser Coup.

A Strange Film Adventure (Bilbao on a hot day . . .)

MG   *Topical Times*, 520, 2 Nov. 1929. A Strange Film Adventure.

The Girl from Gibraltar (Baltimore Jones had cleaned . . .)

MG   *Topical Times*, 530, 11 Jan. 1930. The Girl from Gibraltar.

A Gambling Raid (The Mixer and his secretary . . .)

The Silk Stockings (Brighton became a little . . .)

MG   *Topical Times*, 531, 18 Jan. 1930. The Silk Stockings.

The Case of Dolly de Mulle (The Mixer's business . . .)

MG   *Topical Times*, 536, 22 Feb. 1930. The Case of Dolly de Mulle.

The Seventy-fourth Diamond (The stolid-looking Inspector . . .)

MG   *Topical Times*, 532, 25 Jan. 1930. The Seventy-fourth Diamond.

CINEMA TEACHING BY POST (I notice, said Paul . . .)

THE BILLITER BANK SMASH (It was whilst the Mixer . . .)

THE SPANISH PRISONER (Walking one Sunday . . .)

MG   *Topical Times*, 535, 15 Feb. 1930. The Spanish Prisoner.

THE CROWN JEWELS (Sandy had once confided . . .)

MG   *Topical Times*, 534, 8 Feb. 1930. The Crown Jewels.

THE PROFESSOR (The Anglo-American Sugar . . .)

MG   *Topical Times*, 537, 1 Mar. 1930. The Professor.

SS   113   **More Educated Evans**
Webster Publications 1926; Collins 1930, 1932; Tallis Press 1967.

THE RETURN OF THE NATIVE (It is an axiom . . .)

A SOUVENIR (Through his uncurtained window . . .)

THE MAKER OF WINNERS (The Miller would have passed . . .)

A JUDGE OF RACING (The Honourable Mr. Justice Bellfont . . .)

MG   *E.W.M.M.* (Br.), No. 21, Apr. 1966. A Judge of Racing.

AN AMAZING SELECTION (There is no doubt . . .)

A GOOD GALLOP (Alfred Robspear . . .)
A HORSE OF THE SAME COLOUR (The two-year-old Hesperus . . .)
MIXING IT (Every great man . . .)

N   *Evening Standard*, 4 Jan. 1938. Mixing It.

THE FREAK DINNER (All the world knows . . .)
THE USER OF MEN (By some miracle . . .)
THE LADY WATCHDOG (Satan, the original . . .)
THE JOURNALIST (Mr. Frithington-Evans had a colt . . .)

B114 Mouthpiece, The (By Edgar Wallace & Robert Curtis) (There might have been occasions . . .)
Hutchinson 1935, 1950; Arrow Books 1963.

Murder Book of Mr. J. G. Reeder (See B106)

NF   **B115 My Hollywood Diary** (It is rather sad going away . . .)
Hutchinson 1932.

Mystery of Mary Grier, The (see B98)

B116 Nine Bears, The (Alt. titles: The Other Man; Silenski, Master Criminal; The Cheaters) (Men who think in millions usually . . .)
Ward Lock & Co. 1910, 1928.
Ward Lock 6d. Copyright novels 253.

B117 '1925', The Story of a Fatal Peace ('You don't really believe all that . . .')
George Newnes 1915.

SS   **B118 Nobby** (Alt. titles: Smithy's Friend Nobby)
George Newnes 1916, 1928; Newnes Trench

Library 1917; Newnes New Size Novels, 1928.

C. A. Ransom & Co. Paper Backed novels.

NOBBY'S BEST GIRL (Smithy sat on the canteen table . . .)

MG   *Storyteller*, July 1907. Smithy's Best Girl.

AUTHORSHIP 'Every man,' said Smithy . . .)

MG   *Ideas*, 142, 5 Dec. 1907. Smithy on Authorship.

PRIVATE CLARK'S WILL ('Nobby Clark went to hospital . . .')

ON ADVERTISING ('There was a bit in the paper . . .')

MG   *Ideas*, 145, 26 Dec. 1907. Smithy on Advertising.

ON PROMOTION (Fellers who got on in the world . . .)

MG   *Ideas*, 139, 14 Nov. 1907. Smithy on Promotion.

'No. 2 MAGAZINE' ('Lots of fellows go home for Christmas . . .')

SMITHY—AMBASSADOR ('There's a lot of fun in the army . . .')

MG   *Ideas*, 140, 21 Nov. 1907. Smithy—Ambassador.

HOGMANAY ('Nobby Clark was tellin' . . .'

MG   *Ideas*, 146, 2 Jan. 1908. Smithy on Hogmanay.

ON FINANCE (Private Smith was in a . . .)

MG   *Ideas*, 138, 7 Nov. 1907. Smithy on Finance.

THE HEROES (Being a hero is not much . . .)

MG   *Ideas*, 136, 24 Oct. 1907. Smithy's Band of Heroes.

THE COMPETITORS (Not the least pleasant . . .)
UNCLE JOE'S TRACT ('Nobby Clark,' explained Private Smith . . .)

THE BAA-LAMB (The army is a queer place . . .)

MG   *Ideas*, 150, 1 Feb. 1908. Smithy and the Baa Lamb.

NOBBY'S 'DOUBLE' ('You might say . . .')

MG   *Ideas*, 141, 28 Nov. 1907. Nobby's 'Double'.

THE FIGHTING ANCHESTERS (Once upon a time . . .)

MG   *Ideas*, 137, 31 Oct. 1907. Smithy & the Fighting Anchesters.

SECRET SIGNS (You can find lots of ways . . .)

THE FAITH OF PRIVATE SIMPSON ('You quite understand . . .')

B119 Northing Tramp, The (The tramp looked to be less savoury . . .)
Hodder & Stoughton 1926; Pan Books (The Tramp); Hodder & Stoughton 9d. Yellow Jackets.

B120 Number Six (Alt. title: Number Six and the Borgia)
(The most mysterious and baffling thing . . .)
Newnes New Size Novels 1927; George Newnes 1928, 1928; C. A. Ransom & Co. Paper covered edition.

Number Six and the Borgia (see **B120**)

B121 On the Spot (Tony Perelli was not yellow . . .)
John Long 1931, 1948; Arrow Books 1962, 1955, 1957.

SS **B122 Orator, The**
Hutchinson 1928; Arrow Books 1966.

THE ORATOR (They called Chief Inspector
Oliver Rater ...)

MG *Topical Times*, 487, 16 Mar. 1929. The
Poisoned Cup.

MG *Pall Mall Magazine*, Vol. 1, No. 4, Aug. 1927.
The Orator.

THE MIND-READERS (There is no police force
in the world ...)

MG *Topical Times*, 488, 22 Mar. 1929. The Mind
Readers.

N *Evening Standard*, 5 Aug. 1935. The Mind
Readers.

MG *Pall Mall Magazine*, Vol. 1, No. 6, Oct. 1927.
The Mind Readers.

BK *Fifty Famous Detectives of Fiction*: The Mind
Readers.

THE OLD LADY WHO CHANGED HER MIND
(Mr. Rater never took a job ...)

MG *Topical Times*, 489, 30 Mar. 1929. The Old
Lady who Changed her Mind.

MG *Pall Mall Magazine*, Vol. 1, No. 5, Sept. 1927.
The Old Lady Who Changed her Mind.

THE SUNNINGDALE MURDER (There was a
certain assistant ...)

MG *Topical Times*, 490, 6 Apr. 1929. The Sunningdale Murder.

MG *Pall Mall Magazine*, Vol. 1, No. 8, Dec. 1927.
The Sunningdale Murder.

A BANK & A SECRETARY (The Orator knew
the London & Southern ...)

MG *Topical Times*, 491, 13 Apr. 1929. A Bank & a
Secretary.

MG   *Pall Mall Magazine*, Vol. 1, No. 7. A Bank & a Secretary.

THE MAN NEXT DOOR (When Mr. Giles walked into the . . .)

MG   *Topical Times*, 492, 29 Apr. 1929. The Man Next Door.

MG   *Pall Mall Magazine*, Vol. 1, No. 10, Feb. 1928. The Man Next Door.

THE SIRIUS MAN (The Orator was not in his most . . .)

MG   *E.W.M.M.* (Br.), No. 13, Aug. 1965. The Sirius Man.

MG   *Topical Times*, 493, 27 Apr. 1929. The Sirius Man.

MG   *Pall Mall Magazine*, Vol. 1, No. 9, Jan. 1929. The Sirius Man.

THE COUPER BUCKLE (Inspector Rater had a friend . . .)

MG   *Topical Times*, 494, 4 May 1929. The Couper Buckle.

MG   *Pall Mall Magazine*, Vol. 1, No. 12, Apr. 1928. The Couper Buckle.

THE CASE OF FREDDIE VANE (Inspector Rater very seldom went . . .)

MG   *Topical Times*, 495, 11 May 1929. The Case of Caper Vane.

MG   *Pall Mall Magazine*, Vol. 1, No. 11, Mar. 1928. The First Night.

THE GUY FROM MEMPHIS (There was a society of men and women . . .)

MG   *E.W.M.M.* (Br.) No. 14, Sept. 1965. The Guy from Memphis.

MG   *Topical Times*, 496, 18 May 1929. The Guy from Memphis.

MG   *Pall Mall Magazine*, Vol. 1, No. 13, May

1928. The Guy from Memphis.

THE DETECTIVE WHO TALKED (Let me say at first I was never . . .)

MG   *Topical Times*, 497, 25 May 1929. The Detective who Talked.

MG   *Pall Mall Magazine*, Vol. 1, No. 15, July 1929. The Detective who Talked.

THE FALL OF MR. RATER (The Orator was a man who had very . . .)

MG   *Topical Times*, 498, 1 June 1929. The Fall of Mr. Rater.

MG   *Pall Mall Magazine*, Vol. 1, No. 14, June 1928. The Orator's Downfall.

Other Man, The (see **B116**)

Pallard the Punter (see **B74**)

Park Lane Mystery, The (see **B83**)

B123   **'Penelope' of the Polyantha** (There is a man in London . . .)
Hodder & Stoughton 1926.
Hodder & Stoughton 9d. Yellow Jackets.

NF   B124   **People** (Alt. titles: Edgar Wallace; a Short Biography; Edgar Wallace by himself) (I am aware that this autobiography differs . . .)
Hodder & Stoughton 1926.

SS   B125   **People of the River, The**
Ward Lock & Co. 1912, 1949.

A CERTAIN GAME (Sanders had been away on holiday . . .)

MG   *Weekly Tale Teller*, 155, 20 Aug. 1912. A Certain Game.

THE ELOQUENT WOMAN (There was a woman of the N'gombi . . .)

MG   *Weekly Tale Teller*, 158, 11 May 1912. The Eloquent Woman.

THE AFFAIR OF THE LADY MISSIONARY (The house of De Silva . . .)

MG   *The Weekly Tale Teller*, 156, 27 Apr. 1912. The Affair of the Lady Missionary.

THE SWIFT WALKER (They have a legend in the Akasava . . .)

MG   *Weekly Tale Teller*, 157, 4 May 1912. The Swift Walker.

BRETHREN OF THE ORDER (Native men loved Sanders . . .)

MG   *Weekly Tale Teller*, 160, 25 May 1912. Brethren of the Order.

THE VILLAGE OF IRONS (Sanders was used to the childlike . . .)

MG   *Weekly Tale Teller*, 174, 31 Aug. 1912. In the Village of Irons.

THE THINKER AND THE GUM-TREE (There are three things which are . . .)

MG   *Weekly Tale Teller*, 159, 18 May 1912. The Thinker and the Gum-Tree.

NINE TERRIBLE MEN (There were nine terrible men . . .)

MG   *Weekly Tale Teller*, 173, 24 Aug. 1912. Nine Terrible Men.

THE QUEEN OF THE N'GOMBI (There are certain native traits . . .)

MG   *Weekly Tale Teller*, 176, 14 Sept. 1912. The Queen of N'Gombi.

THE MAN ON THE SPOT (Once upon a time a man . . .)

MG   *Weekly Tale Teller*, 183, 2 Nov. 1912. The Ruler of the River.

THE RISING OF THE AKASAVA (A native alone may plumb . . .)

MG   *Weekly Tale Teller*, 177, 21 Sept. 1912. The Rising of the Akasava.

MG   *Weekly Tale Teller*, 178, Sept. 1912. Mr. Commissioner Bosambo.

THE MISSIONARY (There is a moral story . . .)

MG   *Weekly Tale Teller*, 175, 7 Sept. 1912. Sanders—Missionary.

THE MAKER OF SPEARS (North of the Akasava country . . .)

MG   *Weekly Tale Teller*, 179, 5 Oct. 1912. A Maker of Spears.

THE PRAYING MOOR (Ariboo told Sanders that . . .)

MG   *Weekly Tale Teller*, 181, 19 Oct. 1912. The Teller of Tales.

THE SICKNESS MONGO (Sanders taught his people . . .)

MG   *Weekly Tale Teller*, 180, 12 Oct. 1912. The Sickness Mongo.

THE CRIME OF SANDERS (It is a fine thing to . . .)

MG   *Weekly Tale Teller*, 182, 26 Oct. 1912. The Crime of Sanders.

SPRING OF THE YEAR (The life of one of his Britannic . . .)

MG   *Weekly Tale Teller*, 184, 9 Nov. 1912. Spring of the Year.

LSS   **B126   Planetoid 127**

Readers Library; Mar., Apr. 1929.

Planetoid 127 ('Chap' West, who was never . . .)

MG   *Mechanical Boy*, Nos. 1 to 8, Planetoid 127. 4 Sept. 1924 to 23 Oct. 1924.

MG   *E.W.M.M.* (Br.), No. 5, Dec. 1964. Planetoid 127.

The Sweizer Pump (The directors' office of the firm . . .)

Police Work (see **B65**)

Pool, The (see **B80**)

CSS   **B127**   **Prison-Breakers, The**
George Newnes 1929.
All stories reprinted in Forty Eight Short Stories.

The Prison Breakers (It was the sort of thing . . .)

MG   *E.W.M.M.* (Br.), No. 30; Jan. 1967. The Prison Breakers.

MG   *Thriller*, 288, 11 Aug. 1934. The Prison Breakers.

Findings are Keepings (Findings are keepings . . .)

BK   *The Thief in the Night* (Digit): Findings are Keepings.

BK   *For Information Received*: Findings are Keepings.

The Jewel Box (There were very few moments when . . .)

The Undisclosed Client (A snowy night in early March . . .)

BK	*The Undisclosed Client*: The Undisclosed Client.
	VIA MADEIRA (This story concerns four people . . .)
BK	*The Thief in the Night* (Digit): Via Madeira.
	THE COMPLEAT CRIMINAL (Mr. Felix O'Hara Golbeater . . .)
MG	20 *Story Magazine*, Jan. 1930. The Perfect Criminal.
BK	*The Thief in the Night* (Digit): The Compleat Criminal.
	REDBEARD (One of the most jealously guarded secrets . . .)
	BULFOX ASLEEP (People say that Bulfox was a fool . . .)
MG	*Pearsons Weekly*, 1980, 7 July 1928. A Question of Honour.
MG	20 *Story Magazine*, Jan. 1931. Bulfox Asleep.
MG	*Novel Magazine*, Apr. 1913. A Question of Honour.

B128 **Private Selby** (Probably 'old Cull Grain' . . .)
Ward Lock & Co. 1912, 1930.
Ward Lock 6d. Copyright novels 273.

Proud Sons of Ragusa, The (see B78)

Queen of Sheba's Belt, The (see B66)

Ragged Princess, The (see B48)

LSS B129 **Red Aces**
Hodder & Stoughton 1929; Pan Books 1961, 1962, 1963.

E

	RED ACES (When a young man is very . . .)
MG	*Thriller*, 1, 9 Feb. 1929. Red Aces.

KENNEDY THE CON MAN (The man who stood with . . .)

MG *Thriller*, 3, 23 Feb. 1929. Kennedy the Con Man.

THE CASE OF JOE ATTYMAN (In the dusk of the evening . . .)

SS **B130 Reporter, The** (Alt. title: Wise Y. Symon)
Readers Library 1929; Allied Newspapers in conjunction with Readers Library; New Chevron Series No. 111 1941; Digit 1961, 1962.

THE REPORTER (York Symon was the perfect . . .)

MG *Pearsons Weekly*, 1961, 25 Feb. 1928. The Duchess.

MG *Novel Magazine*, July 1919. The Duchess.

THE WRITINGS OF MACONOCHIE HOE (That Wise Symon was a great . . .)

MG *Pearsons Weekly*, 1965, 24 Mar. 1928. The Writings of Maconochie Hoe.

MG *Novel Magazine*, Oct. 1919. The Writings of Maconochie Hoe.

THE MURDER OF BENNETT SANDMAN (Y. Symon swung his pyjama'd legs . . .)

MG *Pearsons Weekly*, 1959, 11 Feb. 1928. The Murder of Bennett Sandman.

MG *Novel Magazine*, Sept. 1919. The Murder of Bennett Sandman.

THE CRIME OF GAI JOI (Mr. York Symon did not attain . . .)

MG   *Pearsons Weekly*, 1967, 7 Apr. 1928. The Crime of Gai Joi.

MG   *Novel Magazine*, Nov. 1919. The Crime of Gai Joi.

THE LETHBRIDGE ABDUCTION (Do you really want to know . . .)

MG   *Pearsons Weekly*, 1968, 14 Apr. 1929. The Lethbridge Abduction.

MG   *Novel Magazine*, Dec. 1919. The Lethbridge Abduction.

THE SAFE DEPOSIT AT THE SOCIAL CLUB (York Symon Strolled into the . . .)

MG   *Pearsons Weekly*, 1970, 28 Apr. 1928. The Social Club Safe Deposit.

MG   *Novel Magazine*, Jan. 1920. The Social Club Safe Deposit.

THE CASE OF CROOK BERESFORD (Ordinarily, women did not greatly . . .)

MG   *Pearsons Weekly*, 1927, 12 May 1928. The Case of Crook Beresford.

MG   *Novel Magazine*, Feb. 1920. The Case of Crook Beresford.

THE CRIME EXPERT (York Symon was a man without . . .)

MG   *Pearsons Weekly*, 1954, 7 Jan. 1928. The Crime Expert.

MG   *Novel Magazine*, March 1920. The Crime Expert.

THE LAST THROW OF CROOK BERESFORD (The editor sent for Wise Symon . . .)

MG   *Pearsons Weekly*, 1974, 26 May 1928. The Last Throw of Crook Beresford.

MG   *Novel Magazine*, April 1920. The Last Throw of Crook Beresford.

*Ringer, The (see **B65**) (The Assistant Commissioner of Police pressed . . .)
Hodder & Stoughton.
Hodder & Stoughton 9d. Yellow Jackets.
Play: French's acting Edition 1929.
Pan Books 1948, 1950, 1951, 1954.

MG   *Answers*, 2000–2016, 2 Oct. 1926 to 22 Jan. 1927.

Ringer Returns, The (see **B64**)

B131 River of Stars, The (The road from Alebi is a bush . . .)
Ward Lock & Co. 1913, 1930.
Ward Lock 6d. Copyright novels No. 281 1930; Digit 1963.

B132 Room 13 (Over the grim stone archway . . .)
Assoc. Newspapers (not dated); John Long Aug. 1924, 1925, 1967; Arrow 1961; Cherry Tree Books No. 5 1940.

N   *Daily Express*, 12 Mar to 28 Apr. 1923. Room 13.

B133 Sanctuary Island (Novel of film by Robert Curtis) (Anyone who had seen Elizabeth Anson . . .)
Hutchinson 1936.

---

*Although 'The Ringer' is not listed as a separate book, the story has been so rewritten it is almost unrecognisable as the same story. Wallace himself states that this is the story of the play The Ringer based on the novel The Gaunt Stranger. It is interesting to note that The Gaunt Stranger was dedicated to P. G. Wodehouse and The Ringer was dedicated to Sir Gerald Du Maurier.

SS **B134 Sanders** (Alt. title: Mr. Commissioner Sanders)
Hodder & Stoughton March 1926; July 1954, 1964; Hodder & Stoughton 9d. Yellow Jackets.
Pan Books 1948.

THE MAGIC OF FEAR (All this happened in the interim . . .)

MG *Saint Magazine* (Br.), Nov. 1964. The Magic of Fear.

MG Presumed *Grand Magazine*.

THE CLEAN SWEEPER (The soldiers of the old King who . . .)

MG *Grand Magazine*, Vol. 47, Mar to Aug. 1925. Bones & the Magic Music.

THE VERY GOOD MAN (The spectacle of a white man . . .)

MG *Grand Magazine*, Vol. 48, Sept. 1925 to Feb. 1926. Bones & The Qualified Nurse.

WOMEN WILL TALK (If you hack down a copal tree . . .)

MG Presumed *Grand Magazine*.

THE SAINT (From time to time there passed . . .)

MG *Grand Magazine*, Vol. 49, Mar to Aug. 1926. Bones & the Saint.

THE MAN WHO HATED SHEFFIELD (Beyond the forest of happy dreams . . .)

MG *Grand Magazine*, Vol. 48, Sept. 1925 to Feb. 1926. Bones & the Gold Seeker.

THE JOY SEEKERS (The Zaire had once paid a visit . . .)

MG Presumed *Grand Magazine*.

THE BALL GAME (Doran Campbell-Cairns was very kind . . .)

MG   *Grand Magazine*, Vol. 48, Sept. 1925 to Feb. 1926. Bones Proposes.

THE WISE MAN (At rare intervals, once in a . . .
MG   *Grand Magazine*, Vol. 48, Sept. 1925 to Feb. 1926. Bones & the Ghost men.

THE SWEET SINGER (When Lieutenant Tibbets had a great educational . . .)
MG   *Grand Magazine*, Vol. 48, Sept. 1925 to Feb. 1926. The Capture of Bones.

SS   **B135** **Sanders of the River**
Ward Lock & Co. 1911, 1918, 1933; Digit 1963.

THE EDUCATION OF THE KING (Mr. Commissioner Sanders had graduated . . .)
MG   *Novel Magazine*, Feb. 1912. The Education of the King.
MG   *Weekly Tale Teller*, 38, 22 Jan 1910. The Exploiter.
MG   *Weekly Tale Teller*, 43, 26 Feb. 1910. The Education of King Peter.

KEEPERS OF THE STONE (There is a people who live at Ochori . . .)
MG   *Weekly Tale Teller*, 51, 23 Apr. 1910. The Keepers of the Stone.

BOSAMBO OF MONROVIA (For many years have the Ochori . . .)
MG   *Weekly Tale Teller*, 46, 19 Mar. 1910. Bosambo of Monravia.

THE DROWSY ONE (There were occasions when Sanders . . .)

THE SPECIAL COMMISSIONER (The Hon. George Tackle had the . . .)

MG   *Weekly Tale Teller*, 29, 20 Nov. 1909. The Special Commissioner.

THE DANCING STONES (Heroes should be tall and . . .)

MG   *Weekly Tale Teller*, 66, 6 Aug. 1910. The Dancing Stones.

THE FOREST OF HAPPY DREAMS (Sanders was tied up at a . . .)

THE AKASAVAS (You who do not understand . . .)

MG   *Weekly Tale Teller*, 107, 20 May 1911. The Akasavas.

THE WOOD OF DEVILS (Four days out of M'Sakidanga . . .)

MG   *Weekly Tale Teller*, 21, 25 Sept. 1909. The Wood of Devils.

THE LOVES OF M'LINO (When a man loves a woman . . .)

MG   *Weekly Tale Teller*, 103, 22 Apr. 1911. The Loves of M'Lino.

THE WITCH DOCTOR (Nothing surprised Sanders . . .)

MG   *Weekly Tale Teller*, 98, 18 Mar. 1911. The Devil Man.

THE LONELY ONE (Mr. Commissioner Sanders had lived . . .)

MG   *Weekly Tale Teller*, 128, 14 Oct. 1911. The Lonely One.

THE SEER (There are many things that happen . . .)

MG   *Weekly Tale Teller*, 133, 18 Nov. 1911. The Telepathist.

DOGS OF WAR (Chiefest of the Restrictions. . .)

MG   *Weekly Tale Teller*, 63, 16 July 1910. **Dogs of War.**

B136 Sandi the King Maker (In the village of P'pie at the foot . . .)
Ward Lock & Co. 1922; Digit 1963.

MG   *Windsor Magazine*, Vol. 53 & 54, Dec. 1920 to Nov. 1921.

Scotland Yard's Yankee Dick (see **B168**)

B137 Secret House, The (A man stood irresolutely . . .)
Ward Lock & Co. 1917, 1951; Digit 1963.

SS **B138 Sergeant Sir Peter** (Alt. title: Sergeant Dunn C.I.D.)
Chapman & Hall 1932; George Newnes 1933.

    *1. THE FOUR MISSING MERCHANTS (Peter Dunn walked into his . . .)
MG   *Strand Magazine* Dec. 1929. **The Four Missing Merchants.**

    2. THE DESK BREAKER (There is a regular and steady . . .)
MG   *Strand Magazine*, Jan. 1930, Vol. ? **The Desk Breaker.**

    3. THE INHERITOR (Any country is a pretty small . . .)
MG   *Strand Magazine*, Feb. 1930, Vol. ? **The Inheritor.**

    4. DR. FIFER'S PATIENT (Yours, sir, must be an interesting . . .)

*Layout of chapters in SERGEANT DUNN C.I.D.

Sergeant Dunn C.I.D.

MG   *Strand Magazine*, Mar. 1930, Vol.? Dr. Fifer's Patient.

5. THE BURGLAR ALARM (Superintendent Leigh of the Criminal . . .)

MG   *Strand Magazine*, Apr. 1930, Vol.? The Burglar Alarm.

6. BURIED TREASURE (There is water is the Great . . .)

MG   *Strand Magazine*, May 1930, Vol.? Buried Treasure.

MG   *Saint Magazine* (Br.), **July** 1959. The Deadly Mr. Lyon.

7. THE PRINCIPLES OF JO LOLESS (Long before Peter Dunn had . . .)

MG   *Strand Magazine*, June 1930, Vol. ? The Principles of Jo Lawless.

8–13. THE DEATH WATCH (Lee Smitt had no Police record . . .)
(J. G. Reeder mentioned)

MG   *Thriller*, 158, 13 Feb. 1932. The Death Watch.

Sergeant Dunn C.I.D. (see **B138**)
Digit Books 1962: Chapters not titled although a series of exploits; see 'Sergeant Sir Peter' for layout of chapters.

Sign of the Leopard, The (see **B145**)

Silenski, Master Criminal (see **B116**)

Silver Key, The (see **B30**)

Silver Steel (see **B40**)

Sinister Halls (see **B42**)

B139 **Sinister Man, The** ('You have beauty', said
Mr. Maurice Tarn . . .)
Hodder & Stoughton 1924, abr. 1938.
Hodder & Stoughton 9d. Yellow Jackets.

MG   *Answers*, 1866–1884,1 Mar. to 5 July 1924.
The Sinister Man.

Sinister Street (see **B40**)

Sins of the Mother, The (see **B148**)

SS   **B140** **Smithy** (Alt. title: Smithy, not to mention
Nobby Clark & Spud Murphy)
First appeared in *Daily Mail*; 2nd impression
1905 Tallis Press; George Newnes 1914,
1928; Newnes Trench Library 1917; Newnes
New Size Novels 1926; C. A. Ransom & Co.
Paper covered edition.

THE ADJUTANT'S MADNESS (Military 'crime'
is not a crime at all . . .)

MILITARY MOTORING (What'll be the badge
for that ? . . .)

ADVERTISING THE ARMY (It's a great thing,
getting . . .)

ARMY MANNERS (Officers commanding regiments are . . .)

THE UMPIRE (Smithy sprawled lazily on the
grassy . . .)

ERUDITION (It was read out in reg'mental orders . . .)

BERTIE (You don't happen to know our Bertie . . .)

NOBBY'S PART (I didn't see you at our piece . . .)

THE CLAIRVOYANT (Do you believe in ghosts? . . .)

BOOTS (Young and growing soldiers . . .)

JU-JITSU (Politics form no part of the . . .)

THE NEW OFFICER ('The Officer', said Private Smithy . . .)

THE AGITATOR (Heard about our secret society . . .)

MISSING WORDS (Many years ago a popular periodical . . .)

THE NEW RULES ('You mustn't think', warned Smithy . . .)

THE CHEF ('The thing about the army that's . . .'

THE JOURNALIST (I met Smithy in the High Street . . .)

THE PHOTOGRAPHER (The War Office requests officers . . .)

THE BOOKMAKER ('There's lots of chaps', said Smithy . . .

BACK TO CIVIL LIFE ('It's only nacheral', said Smithy . . .)

*BROTHERS (I myself would be the last man . . .)

*Not included in first edition.

*THE GHOST OF HEILBRON KOPJE (Nobby Clark, by all showing . . .)

*SACRIFICE (According to a man environments . . .)

SS   **B141 Smithy Abroad**: Barrack Room Sketches Edward Hulton Apr. 1909.

THE ARMS STORE (Smithy sat on the edge of . . .)

MG   *Ideas*, 178, 12 Aug. 1908. The Arms Store.

THE BAPTISM OF STEVENS (Those who make a close study . . .)

MG   *Ideas*, 179, 19 Aug. 1908. The Baptism of Stevens.

THE ROTTEN AFFAIR (My knowledge of India being . . .)

MG   *Ideas*, 180, 26 Aug. 1908. The Rotten Affair.

THE BATCHELORS CLUB (Smithy's foreign service covers . . .)

MG   *Ideas*, 181, 2 Sept. 1908. The Batchelors Club.

WHY 'FEATHERWEIGHT JACKSON' ENLISTED (If you complain that I serve . . .)

MG   *Ideas*, 182, 9 Sept. 1908. Why 'Featherweight Jackson' Enlisted.

NOBBY'S LOVE STORY (Some there are who collect . . .)

MG   *Ideas*, 183, 16 Sept. 1908. Smithy's Love Story.

THE CHUCAJEE PLATE (There was once a man, wiser . . .)

MG   *Ideas*, 184, 23 Sept. 1908. The Chucajee Plate.

THE WANDERER (The influence of trade . . .)

MG   *Ideas*, 185, 30 Sept. 1908. The Wanderer.

*Not included in first edition.

THE FIGHT (The learned Erasmus . . .)
MG   *Ideas*, 186, 7 Oct. 1908. The Fight.

THE MISER (Once I walked the mountain-ous . . .)
MG   *Ideas*, 187, 14 Oct. 1908. The Miser.

NOBBY, LTD. I have every reason to believe . . .)
MG   *Ideas*, 188, 21 Oct. 1908. Nobby Ltd.

AN ACT OF WAR (You are very much mis-taken . . .)
MG   *Ideas*, 189, 28 Oct. 1907. An Act of War.

THE FOOTBALL MATCH (I do not deny that the . . .)
MG   *Ideas*, 190, 4 Nov. 1908. The Football Match.

THATCHER'S BROTHER (Superior young non-commissioned . . .)
MG   *Ideas*, 191, 11 Nov. 1908. Thatcher's Brother.

THE INVENTION CRAZE (In compiling military text . . .)
MG   *Ideas*, 192, 18 Nov. 1908. The Invention Craze.

MARSHY, DETECTIVE (It is a fact which my . . .)
MG   *Ideas*, 193, 25 Nov. 1908. Marshy, Detective.

THE GHOST OF THE BROOK (It you add to the title . . .)
MG   *Ideas*, 194, 2 Dec. 1908. The Ghost of the Brook.

SMITHY ON HUMOUR (Sometimes I have the good . . .)
MG   *Ideas*, 195, 9 Dec. 1908. Smithy on Humour.

PIKEY'S LUCK (I associate Smithy with . . .)
MG   *Ideas*, 196, 16 Dec. 1908. Pikey's Luck.

MG		THE BUGLERS (When you are called to . . .) *Ideas*, 197, 23 Dec. 1908. The Buglers.
MG		HONOUR (Of course pickets are . . .) *Ideas*, 198, 30 Dec. 1908. Honour.
MG		SACRIFICE (According to a man's . . .) *Ideas*, 199, 6 Jan. 1909. Sacrifice.
MG		'A SURPRESSED BOOK' ('Nobby clark' said Private Smith . . .) *Ideas*, 200, 13 Jan. 1909. 'A Surpressed Book'.
MG		A SOLDIER & A MAN (Sometimes on cold dark . . .) *Ideas*, 201, 21 Jan. 1909. A Soldier & a Man.

SS **B142** **Smithy & the Hun**
Newnes 1915.

THE MILITARY ANARCHIST ('The worst of being a mug . . .')

THE HEROICS OF PRIVATE PARKER ('I often wonder . . .')

AT MONS (Private Smith came back . . .)

SMITHY ON NEWS (Private Smithy moved . . .)

ON THE LAWYER IN WAR ('What I like', said Smithy . . .)

VON KLUCK'S NEPHEW ('Talking as I was last week . . .)

MG *Town Topics*, 117, 21 Nov. 1914. Von Cluck's Nephew.

ON MEANING WELL ('Nothin',' said Private Smith . . .)

THE PERSEVERING SOLDIER ('There's grand news from Germany . . .')

A DAY WITH THE CROWN PRINCE ('People', said Smithy . . .)

MG   *Town Topics*, 119, 5 Dec. 1914. A Day with the Crown Prince.

NOBBY & THE LAMB ('Id like to meet Zepp'-lin . . .')
NOBBY & THE MISSING ZEP'LINK ('These', said Private Smith . . .)

MG   *Town Topics*, 113, 24 Oct. 1914. Smithy & the missing Zep'link.

ON THE GERMAN FLEET ('If I hadn't been a soldier . . .')
ON W. O. GENIUS ('There's no doubt . . .')
ON RECRUITING ('There was a feller . . .')

MG   *Royal Magazine*, June 1915. On Betting Commissions.
THE STRATEGIST ('W are confronted . . .')

SMITHY SURVEYS THE LAND ('Removed as he is . . .')

MG   *Town Topics*, 109, 26 Sept. 1914. Smithy Surveys the Land.
LIEUTENANT X ('All the news from the front . . .')

THE LETTER WRITER ('Hows them war correspondents . . .')

MG   *Royal Magazine*, Mar. 1915. Nobby Takes to Letter Writing.

THE WEATHER PROPHET ('If you were to ask me . . .')

MG   *Royal Magazine*, Feb. 1915. When Nobby was a Weather Prophet.

THE INTERPRETER ('In this world', said Private Smith . . .)

MG   *Royal Magazine*, Jan. 1915. The Interpreter.
NOBBY IN ROMANTIC VEIN ('Nobby Clark wrote a poem of hate once . . .')

MG   *Royal Magazine*, Apr. 1915. Nobby in Romantic Vein.

Smithy, not to mention Nobby Clark & Spud Murphy (see **B140**)

Smithy's Friend Nobby (see **B118**)

B143 **Smoky Cell** by Robert Curtis (Novel of the play)
(Josephine Brady place the telephone . . .)
Hutchinson 1936.

Souls in Shadows (see **B99**)

B144 **Square Emerald, The** (Alt. titles: The Girl from Scotland Yard; The Woman) (Lady Raytham drew aside the long velvet . . .)
Hodder & Stoughton 1926, 1935.
Hodder & Stoughton 9d. Yellow Jackets.

N   *Daily Express* 13 Nov. to Dec. 1925. The Woman.

B145 **Squeaker, The** (Alt. titles: The Squealer; The Sign of the Leopard) (It was a night that normal . . .)
Hodder & Stoughton 1927; Pan Books 1950.
Hodder & Stoughton 9d Yellow Jackets.

Play: Hodder & Stoughton 1929, Act 1, Scene 1 (A corner of the sub-editor's room on . . .)

Squealer, The (see **B145**)

Stamped in Gold (see **B67**)

NF   **B146**   **Standard History of the War**
George Newnes 1914.

4 vols.
VOL. 1 With Gen. French's Despatches.
VOL. 2 As above.
VOL. 3 St. Eloi, Givenchy, Ypres, Hill 60, Neuve, Chapelle.
VOL. 4 The Navy & the Dardanelles.

SS   **B147**   **Steward, The**
Collins Aug. 1932, Sept. 1932, Mar. 1933, July 1933, May 1934.

THE STEWARD & THE SHARPS (You must imagine the . . .)
OVERDUE (I am telling you . . .)
THE BUOY THAT DID NOT LIGHT (What's that word that . . .)
THE LEFT PASS (There was a lady artist . . .)

MG   *Pall Mall Magazine*, No. 20, Dec. 1928. The Left Pass.

THE GHOST OF JOHN HOLLING (There are things about . . .)
MG   *Grand Magazine*, Vol. 45, Mar. to Aug. 1924. The Ghost of John Holling.

THE LITTLE BARONESS (When you're twenty one . . .)
MG   *Saint Magazine* (Br.), May 1964. The Little Baroness.
MG   *Grand Magazine*, Vol. 49, Mar. to Aug. 1926. The Little Baroness.

SOLO & THE LADY (I'm naturally fond of . . .)

MG   20 *Story Magazine*, Oct. 1924. Solo & the Lady.

THE BARONS OF THE NIMBLE PACK (In the old days . . .)

MG   *Grand Magazine* Vol. 41, Mar. to Aug. 1922. Lords of the Nimble Pack.

B148 Strange Countess, The (Alt. title: The Sins of the Mother) (Lois Margeritta Reddle sat on the edge . . .)
Hodder & Stoughton 1925.
Hodder & Stoughton 9d Yellow Jackets.

Sweizer Pump, The (see **B126**)

B149 Table, The by Robert Curtis (Novel of the Hollywood horror film) (Three times within three minutes . . .)
Hutchinson 1936.

Take-a-Chance Anderson (see **B111**)

Tam (see **B150**)
Newnes New Size Novels 1928.
C. A. Ransome & Co. Paperback edition.

B150 Tam of the Scouts (Alt. title; Tam)
George Newnes 1918 written originally for the American Market.

  *Chapter 1. (Lieutenant Bridgeman had gone out . . .)
Chapter 2. ('Whaur's Tam?—Tam's awa' . . .)

*Chapters Listed as they are believed to have been re-printed individually.

Chapter 3. (There arrived at the aerodrome ...)

Chapter 4. (On the earth rain was falling ...)

Chapter 5. ('I hae noticed', said Tam o' the Scouts ...)

Chapter 6. ('Some people say that the German ...'

Chapter 7. (Sergeant-Pilot Tam struck a bad patch ...)

Chapter 8. (Tam stood in the doorway of Squadron ...)

Chapter 9. (There are certain persons, animals, and ...)

Chapter 10. (Along a muddy road came an ambulance ...)

B151 Terrible People, The (Alt. title: The Gallows' Hand) (Harry the Lancer came into Burton ...)

N *The People* 6 Dec. 1925 to 23 May 1926. The Gallows' Hand.
Hodder & Stoughton 1926 abr. 1938.
Hodder & Stoughton 9d Yellow Jackets.

B152 Terror, The
Collins 1929, 1930: Hodder & Stoughton 1929 (Play); Digit 1962.

THE TERROR (O'Shea was in his maddest mood ...)

*THE CAT BURGLAR (Old Tom Burkes used to say ...)

BK *Forty Eight Short Stories*: The Cat Burglar.

*In Digit Publications only.

BK   *The Cat Burglar*: The Cat Burglar.

            *THE STRETELLI CASE (Detective Inspector John Mackenzie . . .)

BK   *The Little Green Man*: The Stretelli Case.
BK   *Forty Eight Short Stories*: The Stretelli Case.
MG   *Thriller*, 286, 28 July 1934. The Stretelli Case.

B153 Terror Keep (Rightly speaking it is improper . . .)
Hodder & Stoughton May 1927: Pan Books 1964.

B154 Thief in the Night, The (. . . Also ask your wife where she . . .) Readers Library Nov. 1928; *Digit1962.
Note
This edition contained the following stories:
THE THIEF IN THE NIGHT (. . . also ask your wife where she . . .)

VIA MADEIRA (This story concerns four people . . .)

BK   *Forty Eight Short Stories*. Via Madeira.
BK   *The Prison Breakers*. Via Madeira.

THE GREEK POROPULOS (At Carolina in the Transvaal . . .)

BK   *Forty Eight Short Stories*. The Greek Poropulos.
BK   *The Governor of Chi-Foo*. The Greek Poropulos.

MG   *Weekly Tale Teller*, 81, 19 Nov. 1910. The Greek Poropulos.

MG   *E.W.M.M.* (Br.) No. 23, June 1966. The Killer of Lioska.

*In Digit Publications only.

FINDINGS ARE KEEPINGS (Findings are Keepings . . .)

BK   *Forty Eight Short Stories*. Findings are Keepings.

BK   *For Information Received*. Findings are Keepings.

BK   *The Prison Breakers*. Findings are Keepings.

THE COMPLEAT CRIMINAL (Mr. Felix O'Hara Golbeater. . .)

BK   *Forty Eight Short Stories*. The Compleat Criminal.

MG   20 *Story Magazine* Jan. 1930. The Perfect Criminal.

BK   *The Prison Breakers*. The Compleat Criminal.

THE LOOKER & THE LEAPER (Foley, the smoke room oracle. . .)

BK   *Forty Eight Short Stories*. The Looker & the Leaper.

BK   *Circumstantial Evidence*. The Looker & the Leaper.

CSS **B155** **This England:** Collection of very short articles written in story form from the *Morning Post*, dealing with characters in our English way of life.

Hodder & Stoughton 1927.

THE CRASHED (I stopped my car before . . .)

THE IDLE RICH (My friend the Communist . . .)

THE IMPOSSIBLE PEOPLE (He isn't a tramp . . .)

OUR BURGLARS (Nothing gives Bill a . . .)

THE SURGEON (Small boys without . . .)

COMMONPLACE PEOPLE (You lose an awful lot . . .)

THE PRECARIOUS GAME (A pretty little house on . . .)

PARSONS (Parsons . . . ? One does not know . . .)

BACK TO THE ARMY ('To the old village . . .)
THE MODERN GIRL (That is about the silliest . . .)
MUSHERS & RIDERS (The musher got his cab. . .)
99, SOMETHING CRESCENT (The curtains that cover . . .)
POLICE (The policeman stands aloof . . .)
THE FARMER (The snow it fell down . . .)
LEARNING TO LEARN (About popular education . . .)
NANNY (The newest addition to . . .)
QUEEN CHARLOTTE'S (A very nice woman got out . . .)
SEA TALK (It occurred to me that . . .)
CONSIDER YOUR VERDICT (It is a terrible bore being . . .)
COMRADES (My communist friend sneers . . .)

B156 Those Folk of Bulboro (My dear Tony, I have addressed . . .)
Ward Lock & Co. 1918, 1936; Digit 1964.

B157 Three Just Men, The (£520 p.a. wanted at once, Laboratory Secretary . . .)
Hodder & Stoughton 1926, 1928, 1950.
Hodder & Stoughton 9d. Yellow Jackets.
MG   *Union Jack*, 1204–1219, 13 Nov. 1926 to 28 Feb. 1927. The Three Just Men.

B158 Three Oak Mystery, The (Murder is neither an art . . .)
Ward Lock & Co. 1924; Digit 1963.
N   *Daily Express* 5 July to Aug. 1921.

B159 Tomb of T'sin, The (A man walked carelessly through . . .)
Ward Lock & Co. 1916.

B160 Traitor's Gate, The (Guu-a-a-ard! Slope-Hime!...)
Hodder & Stoughton 1927, Sept. 1951, 1956.

B161 Twister, The (In the summer of nineteen-twenty something...)
John Long 1928 (Apr. 1966 revised); Arrow 1962 rev.; Universal Library 1929; Cherry Tree Books No. 28 1938;

N *News of the World*, 4373–4384, 21 Aug. to 6 Nov. 1927. The Twister.

CSS **B162 Undisclosed Client, The**
Digit 1963.

The Undisclosed Client (A snowy night in early March...)
BK *The Prison Breakers*. The Undisclosed Client.
BK *Forty Eight Short Stories*. The Undislosed Client.

The Little Green Man (An understanding disturbed or terminated...)
BK *The Little Green Man*. The Little Green Man.
BK *Forty-Eight Short Stories*. The Little Green Man.

The Governor of Chi-Foo (Chi-Foo as in the Forbidden...)
BK *The Governor of Chi-Foo*. The Governor of Chi-Foo.
BK *Forty Eight Short Stories*. The Governor of Chi-Foo.

The Christmas Cup (Colonel Desboro was an easy...)

135

MG	*Windsor Magazine*, Vol. 63, Dec. 1925 to May 1926. The Christmas Cup.
MG	*E.W.M.M.* (Br.), No. 29, Dec. 1966. The Christmas Cup.
BK	*Fighting Snub Reilly*. The Christmas Cup.
BK	*Forty Eight Short Stories*. The Christmas Cup.
MG	*Royal Magazine*, 1929. He Who Could Ride.

*MR. SIMMONS' PROFESSION (The magistrate looked over . . .)

MG	*Ideas*, 1239, 8 Dec. 1928. Mr. Simmon's Profession.
MG	*Ideas*, 202, 27 Jan. 1904. Mr. Simmon's Profession.

*CHANGE (One of the rummiest fellers . . .)

BK	Rewrite of *A Lady Called Nita*, Mr. Sigee's Relations.
MG	*E.W.M.M.* (Br.), No. 15. Oct. 1965. Duo in Blue.
MG	*Ideas*, 209, 17 Mar. 1909. Change.

*HOW HE LOST HIS MOUSTACHE (Ladies said P.C. Lee . . .)

MG	*Ideas*, 206, 24 Feb. 1909. How He Lost His Moustache.

*SERGEANT RUN-A-MILE (The police force said P.C. Lee . . .)

MG	*Ideas*, 1243, 5 Jan. 1929. The Courtship of Sergeant Run-a-Mile.
MG	*Ideas*, 207, 3 Mar. 1909. Sergeant Run-a-Mile.

*THE SENTIMENTAL BURGLAR (I was wonderin my mind . . .)

MG	*Ideas*, 208, 10 Mar. 1909. The Sentimental Burglar.
MG	*E.W.M.M.* (Br.), 15 Oct. 1965. Duo in Blue.

*Stories of real policemen.

	*PEAR DROPS (P.C. Lee has never struck me . . .)
MG	*Ideas*, 205 17 Feb. 1909. Pear Drops.
	*CONTEMPT (Six years ago I sat in the . . .)
MG	*Ideas*, 1247, 2 Feb. 1929. When the Jury came to Blows.
MG	*Ideas*, 211, 31 Mar. 1909. Contempt.
	*A MAN OF NOTE (Once I hinted delicately to . . .)
MG	*Ideas*, 203, 3 Feb. 1909. A Man of Note.
	*FOR JEWEYS LAGGIN (People get queer notions . . .)
MG	*Ideas*, 1240, 15 Dec. 1928. Jeweys Laggin.
MG	*Ideas*, 204, 10 Feb. 1909. For Jeweys Laggin.

NF   **B163 Unofficial Dispatches. War articles** (about 2,000 issued) Reprinted from the *Daily Mail*. Hutchinson Dec. 1901.

THE CITY OF REFUGE (After you have left the ship . . .)

THE FABRIC OF HATE (As South African towns go . . .)

THE REBEL & THE PSALMIST (I have been to church . . .)

THE RAIN THAT STOPPED DE WET (It was a travel-worn . . .)

DE WET'S PLAN (There is a culvert . . .)

PRICES OF PEACE (There have been two . . .)

TO ARMS! (You would think it was . . .)

AMATEUR DE WETS (Matjesfontein is the green . . .)

THE BIRTH OF A CORPS (You may be pardoned . . .)

*Stories of real policemen.

THE SHADOW OVER THE LAND (For many days has the . . .)

THE BETTER PATH (It was at the trial . . .)

THE COMING OF DE WET (The squeal of brakes . . .)

PLUMERS FIGHT (The burley storekeeper . . .)

HOMEWARD BOUND (When I was at . . .)

THE LAST FIGHT ('See! They run!' . . .)

WHY WE LOST DE WET (De Wet being now safely . . .)

PROFIT & LOSS (De Wet has now gone . . .)

A NICE WAR (In the years that are . . .)

TRAGEDY (Evening at De Var . . .)

THAT VICTORIAN (The S.M.O.—which in plain . . .)

DOING NOTHING (We cannot be always . . .)

'PREVIOUSLY UNREPORTED' (Because there are so many . . .)

ATKINS (Such a night as can . . .)

A VELDT ALDERSHOT (What is there about . . .)

THAT TIRED FEELING! (It would be ridiculous . . .)

A SUNDAY MORNING CITY (A mine to the left . . .)

AMERICA'S BID FOR THE RAND (Trade follows the flag . . .)

SOPS TO SENTIMENT ('Mr. Van Nieuenhoys, the . . .)

IN DEATH'S EYE (Of Atkins 'doing nothing' . . .)

A DAY IN KENT! (Let us make holiday . . .)

'CANNOT ACCEPT RESPONSIBILITY' (It was in answer . . .)

TIPS THAT PASS IN THE NIGHT (Note: Lest this letter. . .)

TRUMPS WITHOUT HONOURS (The other day I met . . .)

THE INTERVENING BLACK (And what time Anglophobe . . .)

HEROES OF THE COTTON WASTE (If you cannot find . . .)

Has Kitchener Failed.

RECONSTRUCTING AN ESTIMATE (Whichever party sits on . . .)

FORCES DESPISED (I will not refer at. . .)

REBELLION MADE EASY (At no period, either . . .)

RELATED JUSTICE (When a man gives you . . .)

THE COMING STRUGGLE (Public opinion will, I think . . .)

WHAT SHALL BE THE VERDICT? (I have cited what I . . .)

B164 Valley of Ghosts, The (Fate and an easy running . . .)
Hodder & Stoughton Mar. 1925, June 1941, 1953, rev. ed. 1967; Odhams 1922; Pan Books 1959.

MG   *Pan*, May 1922 to Jan. 1923. The Valley of Ghosts.

V   **B165 War & Other Poems**
1900.
Eastern Press Series No. 1.
These were published in the form of broad-

sheets and only the first sheet was by Edgar Wallace.

1. WAR (A tent that is pitched at the . . .)

2. AFTER (The fight was done an hour ago . . .)

3. THE OLD RULE, 'BRITANNIA'S LAMENT'. (It was a nation new . . .)

4. UNDER WHICH FLAG (Under which flag . . .)

5. THE ARMOURED TRAIN (There's a risk on the . . .)

NF   **B166 War of the Nations**
Newnes. 9 vols. in set but the first vol. was not by Edgar Wallace.

VOLS. 2–4, 1915.
VOLS. 5–7, 1916.
VOLS. 8–9, 1917.

B167 We Shall See (A. The Gaol Breakers) (Shall I write Ichabod across . . .)
Hodder & Stoughton 1926.
Hodder & Stoughton 9d. Yellow Jackets.

B168 When the Gangs Came to London (Alt. titles: Scotland Yard's Yankee Dick; The Gangsters Come to London) (All this began on the day . . .)
John Long 1932, 1946; Readers Library; Arrow Books 1957, 1959.
MG

MG   *Answers*, 2279–2291, 6 Feb to 30 Apr. 1932. When the Gangsters Came to London.

B169 Whiteface (Michael Quigley had a fair working knowledge . . .)
Hodder & Stoughton June 1930, Aug. 1940.
Hodder & Stoughton 9d. Yellow Jackets.

Wireless Bryce (see **B81**)

Wise Y. Simon (see **B130**)

CSS **B170 Woman from the East, The**
Crime Book Society (Hutchinson) 1934; 1952; Digit 1963.

THE WOMAN FROM THE EAST (Overture and beginners please . . .)
THE CHOPHAM AFFAIR (Lawyers who write books are . . .)
Reprinted as THE CHOBHAM AFFAIR, Ellery Queen's Anthology 1964.
THE HOPPER (No. 707, Tressillian Road, is a house . . .)
THE LOVE OF DEVIL HAMPTON (Devil Hampton went out of France . . .)

THE SILVER CHARM (Angel, Esquire, has a little office . . .)
MG *Story Teller*, June 1910. The Silver Charm.
MG *Harmsworth's All Story Magazine*, Aug. 1927. The Silver Charm.

UNCLE FARAWAY (It was thirty years since . . .)
MG *Story Teller*, July 1913. Uncle Faraway.

THE MAN OF THE NIGHT (The little instrument on the table . . .)
MG *Weekly Tale Teller*, 76, 15 Oct. 1910. The Stranger of the Night.

141

PATRIOTS (When William Moss Haggs, the eminent . . .)
Rewritten story from ADMIRABLE CARFEW.

THE FUTURE LADY SHELHOLME (I met George Callifer at the club . . .)

THE XMAS GIFT (No doubt by that Mr. Grewley . . .)

THE MAN WHOM NOBODY LOVED (There are two ways into . . .)

THE STRANGENESS OF JOAB LASHMERE (It is a tradition amongst . . .)

JIMMY & THE DOUGHNUT (Jimmy confessed to a large . . .)

MG   *Pearsons Weekly*, 1978, 23 June 1928. Jimmy & the Doughnuts.

CONTROL NO. 2 (Dr. Nischkin made several interesting . . .)

Women, The (see **B144**)

Wolves of the Waterfront (see **B80**)

V   **B171 Writ in Barracks**
Methuen 1900; about 2,000 issued.

WAR.

ARMY DOCTOR.

NICHOLSON'S NEK.

MY PAL—THE BOER.

SONG OF THE FIRST TRAIN THROUGH.

THE NAVAL BRIGADE.

THE ARMOURED TRAIN.

MAKE YOUR OWN ARRANGEMENTS.

GINGER JAMES.

HER MAJESTY HAS BEEN PLEASED.

ARTHUR.

LEGACIES.

T.A. IN LOVE.

TOMMY ADVISES.

THE NUMBER ONE.

BRITANNIA TO HER FIRST-BORN.

TOMMY TO HIS LOUREALE.

THE MISSION THAT FAILED.

THE PRAYER.

CEASE FIRE.

TOMMY'S AUTOGRAPH.

AT THE BRINK.

THE KING OF OOJEE-MOOJEE.

THE SONG OF THE TOWN.

BY SIMONS BAY.

THE SQUIRE.

THE SEA NATION.

NATURE FAILS.

THE COLONEL'S GARDEN.

THE PEOPLE OF CECIL JOHN RHODES.

WHEN LONDON CALLS (July 18th 1899).

CAIROWARDS.

ODE TO THE OPENING OF THE SOUTH AFRICAN EXHIBITION 1898.

B172 Yellow Snake, The (Alt. title: The Black Tenth) (There was no house in Siangtun . . .) Hodder & Stoughton 1926; Pan Books 1960, 1961.
Hodder & Stoughton 9d. Yellow Jackets.

AUTOBIOGRAPHIES & BIOGRAPHIES

Edgar Wallace by Margaret Lane (Greenwich in the seventies . . .)
W. Heinemann Oct. 1938.
Revised and reprinted 1965.
Dedicated to Bryan

Edgar Wallace by his Wife (Ethel V. Wallace)
(After almost seventeen years of . . .)
Hutchinson 1932.

Edgar Wallace Each Way by Robert Curtis
(Edgar Wallace did not write his most thrilling story; he lived it . . .)
John Long 1932.

The Secret of My Successful Marriage by Mrs. Edgar Wallace.
John Long 1930.

The following are already included in main list:

People by Edgar Wallace. Title changed to Edgar Wallace by Edgar Wallace (I am aware that this autobiography differs . . .)
Hodder & Stoughton 1926.
Dedicated to The Rt. Hon. the Earl of Derby KG.

My Hollywood Diary by Edgar Wallace (It is rather sad going away . . .)
Hutchinson 1932.

COLLECTIONS OF STORIES

All details of first lines and shorts are shown elsewhere in catalogue under original publication of novel.

Black, The
Queensway Press 1935.

THE REPORTER.
THE IRON GRIP.

An Edgar Wallace Foursome
John Long 1933.

THE MAN FROM MOROCCO.
CAPTAINS OF SOULS.
THE HAND OF POWER.
THE MIXER.

Edgar Wallace's Police Van
Hodder & Stoughton 1930.

THE GREEN ARCHER.
THE FORGER.
THE DOUBLE.
THE FLYING SQUAD.

The Edgar Wallace Race Special
Collins 1932.

EDUCATED EVANS.
MORE EDUCATED EVANS.
GOOD EVANS.
THE CALENDAR.

Edgar Wallace Second Book: Four Complete Novels.

George Newnes 1931.
NOBBY.
SMITHY.
TAM.
BONES OF THE RIVER.

The Edgar Wallace Souvenir Book
George Newnes 1933.

THE FOUR JUST MEN.
EVE'S ISLAND.
THE CLUE OF THE TWISTED CANDLE.
THE MAN WHO KNEW.

The Educated Man—Good Evans
London Book Co. Novel Library (Collins) 1929.

EDUCATED EVANS.
MORE EDUCATED EVANS.
GOOD EVANS.

Four Complete Novels
George Newnes 1930.

THE FOUR JUST MEN.
EVE'S ISLAND.
THE CLUE OF THE TWISTED CANDLE.
THE MAN WHO KNEW.

EDGAR WALLACE STORIES IN SHORT STORY COLLECTIONS

All details of first lines etc. shown elsewhere in catalogue under original publication of novel.

Four Great Mystery Novels
Odhams 1938.

THE TERROR.

Ellery Queen's Anthology.
Davis Publications, New York, distributed in Great Britain 1964.

THE CHOBHAM AFFAIR (There was a man who had a way with women . . .)
Reprint of The Chopham Affair from THE WOMAN FROM THE EAST starting at the second paragraph.

Rogues Gallery, edited by Ellery Queen.
Faber & Faber 1947.

THE SEVENTY-FOURTH DIAMOND.
Reprinted from THE MIXER.

Fifty Masterpieces of Mystery
Odhams Press. Not dated.

THE CLUE OF MONDAYS SETTLING.
Reprinted from THE CAT BURGLAR. (Note the girl in story is called May Antrim although when story was later reprinted in *E.W.M.M.* (Br.) No. 8 she was called Ann Holter.)

Famous Crimes of Recent Times
C. A. Pearson. Not dated.

1. THE SECRET OF THE MOAT FARM (At the age of fifty-six . . .)
(Dougal)
2. THE MURDER ON YARMOUTH SANDS (The murders committed by criminals . . .)
(Bennett)
3. HERBERT ARMSTRONG, POISONER (The little village of Cusop on the . . .)
(Armstrong)
4. THE TRIAL OF THE SEDDONS (Seddon was essentially a business . . .)
(Seddon)

1, 2, 4 reprinted in *The New Strand*
1, 2, 4 reprinted in *Newnes Crime—True Mystery Series*.
3. reprinted in *Crime and Detection*, No. 1.

The Legion Book
Cassell 1929.

THOMAS ATKINS (article) (Old Soldiers may die, but their . . .)

Fifty Famous Detectives of Fiction
Odhams. Not dated.

THE POETICAL POLICEMAN.
BK · · · · *The Mind of Mr. J. G. Reeder*. The Poetical Policeman.
MG · · · · *Thriller*, 304, 1 Dec. 1934. The Poet Policeman.

MG   *Grand Magazine*, Vol. 46, Sept. 1924 to Feb. 1925. The Strange Case of the Night Watchman.

MG   *Saint Magazine* (Br.), Sept. 1955. The Poetical Policeman.

THE MIND READERS.

BK   *The Orator*. The Mind Readers.

MG   *Topical Times*, 488, 23 1929. The Mind Readers.

MG   *Pall Mall Magazine*, Vol. 1, No. 6, Oct. 1927. The Mind Readers.

N   *Evening Standard*, 5 Aug. 1935. The Mind Readers.

Black Cap: ed. by Cynthia Asquith, Hutchinson 1927.

CIRCUMSTANTIAL EVIDENCE (Colonel Chartres Dane lingered . . .)

BK   *Circumstantial Evidence*. Circumstantial Evidence.

BK   *Forty Eight Short Stories*. Circumstantial Evidence.

MG   *Strand Magazine*, Aug. 1922. Circumstantial Evidence.

MG   *E.W.M.M.* (Br.), No. 9, Apr. 1965. Circumstantial Evidence.

PLAYS OF EDGAR WALLACE

included in collections.

One-Act Play Parade
Allen & Unwin 1935.

THE FOREST OF HAPPY DREAMS (The Forest of N'Bolimi
. . .)
(Sanders)

Play Editions Omnibus
Hodder & Stoughton 1929.

THE MAN WHO CHANGED HIS NAME.

TRUE CRIME

Newnes 1966 **True Crime & Mystery Series**

THE TRIAL OF THE SEDDONS and other stories by other authors.
(Seddon was essentially a business . . .)
THE SECRET OF MOAT FARM and other stories by other authors.
(At the age of fifty-six . . .)
THE MURDER ON YARMOUTH SANDS and other stories by other authors.
(The murders committed by criminals . . .)
All reprinted from FAMOUS CRIMES OF RECENT TIMES; all also published in the *New Strand*.

The Trial of Herbert John Bennett (Introduction by Edgar Wallace) 1929.

The Trial of Patrick Mahon (Introduction by Edgar Wallace 1928.

Crime and Detection No. 1
Tallis Press, June 1966.

The Armstrong Case.
Previously published in FAMOUS CRIMES OF RECENT TIMES.

MISCELLANEA

The Edgar Wallace & Merian C. Cooper Novelisations by Delos W. Lovelace.

King Kong (Even in the obscuring twilight . . .)
Grosset & Dunlap 1932 (U.S.A.)
Corgi 1966.

MG   *Famous Monsters of Filmland*

The Man in the Ditch
This was a record spoken by Edgar Wallace in 1928. Columbia 5026 A 7885–6. A printed copy of this was handed out at the Edgar Wallace Exhibition. ('I was returning from Cheltenham by road . . .')

© Edgar Wallace Ltd. 1965.

MAGAZINES & NEWSPAPERS CONTAINING WORKS BY EDGAR WALLACE LISTED IN THE BIBLIOGRAPHY

All Sports	Serials
Answers	Serials
Boys Favourite	Serials
Chums	Short stories
Daily Express	Serials & articles
Detective Magazine	Serials
Edgar Wallace Mystery Magazine	Short stories & serial
Evening Standard	Short stories
Grand Magazine	Short stories & serials
Happy Magazine	Short stories & serial
Harmsworth All Story Magazine	Short story
Ideas	Short stories, serials & articles
John Bull	Short stories
John Bull Annuals	Short stories
London Calling	Articles
London Mail	Article
Mechanical Boy	Serial
Merry Magazine	Short stories
Nash's Illustrated Weekly	Short stories
New London Magazine	Article
News of the World	Serials & article
New Strand	True crime
Novel Magazine	Short stories & serial
Pan	Short stories & serial
Pall Mall Magazine	Short stories
Pearsons Weekly	Short stories, serial & articles

Penny Illustrated Paper	Story
The People	Serials
Premier Magazine	Short stories
Red Magazine	Short stories
Royal Magazine	Short stories & articles
Saint Detective Magazine	Short stories
Sporting Pink Holiday Annual	Poems
Story Teller	Short stories
Strand Magazine	Short stories, serials & articles
Sunday Graphic and Sunday News	Short stories & articles
Sunday Journal	Serial
Thomsons Weekly News	Short stories & articles
Thriller	Short stories
Topical Times	Short stories
Town Topics	Short stories, articles & poems
20 Story Magazine	Short stories
Union Jack	Serial
Weekly Tale Teller	Short stories
Weekly Telegraph	Serial
Wild West Weekly	Short story
Windsor Magazine	Short stories & article
* *Yes or No.*	Short story

Special Note.

*Information gleaned from a collector who has a single copy.

As mentioned in the foreword Edgar Wallace probably wrote for many others which have not been traced. Apart from '*Yes or No Magazine*', he did contribute to the *Hulton's Christmas Magazine* which are missing from the British Museum. Not taking into account the famous *Daily Mail*, he at one time was contributing articles to almost every National newspaper, as well as his work for the *Birmingham Daily News*.

THE FIRST EDGAR WALLACE STORY PUBLISHED IN A LONDON MAGAZINE

Edgar Wallace in his autobiography PEOPLE published in 1926, stated that 'the first short story I had published in London was based on a "newspaper experience", the wreck of the American boat train at Salisbury which I covered. The story was published in the now defunct *Pall Mall Magazine.*'

This story entitled 'The Barford Snake' was successfully traced, appearing in May 1909. Technically speaking, Edgar Wallace was not strictly correct, as many stories before this date had appeared in *Ideas*. But in all probability he was referring to his first real story, and not 'sketches' as the 'Smithy' and 'Nobby' stories were classed.

Its quite possible of course that there were earlier stories, forgotten by him in the mists of time. If there were, we certainly have found no trace of them in our researches. A close friend of the Wallace family did state in a magazine article that he remembered Edgar Wallace showing him his first story after the First World War. Title of the magazine was not remembered, but it was probably about 1903 and edited by an artist named 'Furniss'. There certainly was an editor named Harry Furniss, who was also a clever illustrator, and who did produce his own magazine called *Lika Jojo* in 1894. Unfortunately, apart from containing no Wallace material, it only ran for one issue. So until proved otherwise the May 1909 must still be accepted as the first.

All Sports (Amalgamated Press)

266–275	27 Sept. to 29 Nov. 1924 LORD DERBY'S RACING MEMORIES BY EDGAR WALLACE.
300–313	23 May to 29 Aug. 1925 THE DOOR WITH SEVEN LOCKS
BK	*The Door with Seven Locks*

Answers (Amalgamated Press).

1665–1676 24 Apr. to 10 July 1920 THE DAFFODIL MURDER
(I don't understand you . . .)
BK *The Daffodil Mystery*

1718–1731 30 Apr. to 30 July 1921 THE DARK EYES OF
LONDON (Larry Holt sat before the Café de . . .)
BK *The Dark Eyes of London*

1743–1769 22 Oct. 1921 to 22 Apr. 1922 BEYOND RECALL:
under pen name of Richard Cloud (Mr.
Septimus Salter pressed the bell . . .)
BK *The Blue Hand*

1847–1866 20 Oct. 1923 to 1 Mar. 1924 SOULS IN SHADOW:
under pen name of Richard Cloud (Lady
Jean Carston reached the bald crest . . .)
BK *The Man from Morocco*

1866–1884 1 Mar. to 5 July 1924 THE SINISTER MAN
(You have beauty, said Mr. Maurice Tarn . . .)
BK *The Sinister Man*

1950–1966 10 Oct. 1925 to 30 Jan. 1926 THE SECOND SON:
under pen name of Richard Cloud (Harry
Alford, eighteenth Earl of Chelford . . .)
BK *The Black Abbot*

2000–2016 2 Oct. 1926 to 22 Jan. 1927 THE RINGER
BK *The Ringer*

2279–2291 6 Feb. to 30 Apr 1932 THE GANGSTERS CAME TO
LONDON
(All this began on the day . . .)
BK *When the Gangs Came to London*

Boys Favourite (Amalgamated Press)

1–11 4 May to 13 July 1929 JACK O' JUDGMENT,
N *Daily Express*, 7. Oct. to 22 Nov. 1919. Jack
o'Judgment.
BK *Jack o'Judgment*

20–33	14 Sept. to 14 Dec. 1929 A KING BY NIGHT
BK	*A King by Night*

Chums (Amalgamated Press)
1927–1928

	ARACHI THE BORROWER (Many years ago the Monrovian . . .)
BK	*Bosambo of the River*. Arachi the Borrower.
MG	*Weekly Tale Teller*, 197, 8 Feb. 1913. Arachi the Borrower.
	THE TAX RESISTERS (Sanders took nothing for granted . . .)
BK	*Bosambo of the River*. The Tax Resisters.
MG	*Weekly Tale Teller*, 201, 8 Mar. 1913. The Tax Resisters.
	THE RISE OF THE EMPEROR (Tobolaka, the King of the Isisi . . .)
BK	*Bosambo of the River*. The Rise of the Emperor.
MG	*Weekly Tale Teller*, 206, 12 Apr. 1913. The Rise of the Emperor.
	THE FALL OF THE EMPEROR (My Poor Soul! said the Houssa . . .)
BK	*Bosambo of the River*. The Fall of the Emperor.
MG	*Weekly Tale Teller*, 207, 19 Apr. 1913. The Fall of Tobolaka.
	THE KILLING OF OLANDI (Chief of Sanders' spies . . .)
BK	*Bosambo of the River*. The Killing of Olandi.
MG	*Weekly Tale Teller*, 213, 31 May 1913. The Killing of Olandi.
	THE PEDOMETER (Bosambo, the Chief of the Ochori . . .)
BK	*Bosambo of the River*. The Pedometer.
MG	*Weekly Tale Teller*, 226, 30 Aug. 1913. The Pedometer.

Edgar Wallace Catalogue

	THE BROTHER OF BOSAMBO (Bosambo was a Monrovian . . .)
BK	*Bosambo of the River*. The Brother of Bosambo.
MG	*Weekly Tale Teller*, 238, 22 Nov. 1913. King of the Ochori.
	THE CHAIR OF N'GOMBI (The N'Gombi people prized . . .)
BK	*Bosambo of the River*. The Chair of the N'Gombi.
MG	*Weekly Tale Teller*, 239, 29 Nov. 1913. The Chair of the N'Gombi.
	THE KI-CHU (The messenger from Sakola . . .)
BK	*Bosambo of the River*. The Ki-Chu.
MG	*Weekly Tale Teller*, 240, 6 Dec. 1913. The Ki- Chu.
	THE CHILD OF SACRIFICE (Out of the waste came a long . . .)
BK	*Bosambo of the River*. The Child of Sacrifice.
MG	*Weekly Tale Teller*, 241, 13 Dec. 1913. The Wonderful Lover.
	THEY (In the Akarti country they . . .)
BK	*Bosambo of the River*. They.
MG	*Weekly Tale Teller*, 242, 20 Dec. 1913. They.
	THE AMBASSADORS (There is a saying amongst the . . .)
BK	*Bosambo of the River*. The Ambassadors.
MG	*Weekly Tale Teller*, 243, 27 Dec. 1913. Bosambo's Devils.
	GUNS IN THE AKASAVA (Thank God! said the Houssa . . .)
BK	*Bosambo of the River*. Guns in the Akasava.

Daily Express

6081–6121 7 Oct. to 22 Nov. 1919 JACK O'JUDGMENT
Started at Chapter 7 with synopsis as previous

158

issues limited in pages due to National rail strike.

BK   *Jack o' Judgment*

MG   *Boys Favourite*, 1–11, 4 May to 13 July 1929. Jack o' Judgment.

5 July to 27 Aug. 1921 THE THREE OAK MYSTERY

BK   *The Three Oak Mystery*

6 Dec. 1921 to 3 Feb. 1922 THE CRIMSON CIRCLE

BK   *The Crimson Circle*

7144–7184   12 Mar. to 28 Mar. 1923 ROOM 13 (Over the grim stone archway . . .)

BK   *Room 13*

7975–8014   13 Nov. to 31 Dec. 1925 THE WOMAN (Lady Raytham drew aside the long . . .)

BK   *The Square Emerald*

9629   16. Mar. 1931 EDGAR WALLACE OFFERS YOU £5,000—to anyone who can prove he had ghosts. (Article)

9629–9659   16 Mar. to 21 Apr. 1931 THE MAN AT THE CARLTON (There was a man named Harry Stone . . .)

BK   *The Man at the Carlton*

Daily Sketch

7008   5 Oct. 1931 I AM HAPPY BECAUSE I AM HEALTHY: Article by Edgar Wallace.

Edgar Wallace Catalogue

The Detective Magazine (Amalgamated Press)
Nos. 1, 2,

3 & 7	Period 24 Nov. 1922 to 16 Feb. 1923 FLAT 2. A £500 prize was offered for the winner who solved the mystery of this story.
BK	*Flat* 2

Nos. 18–31	20 July 1923 to 1 Oct. 1924 THE GREEN ARCHER
BK	*The Green Archer*

Edgar Wallace Mystery Magazine (British)

No. 1.	Aug. 1964 THE GHOST OF DOWN HILL (It was of course a coincidence . . .)
BK	*The Ghost of Down Hill.* The Ghost of Down Hill.

No. 2	Sept. 1964 THIEVES MAKE THIEVES (If you had told Mrs. Cayling . . .)
BK	*Killer Kay.* Thieves Make Thieves.

No. 3	Oct. 1964 BILL OF SCOTLAND YARD (There was a very clever detective . . .)
MG	*Pearsons Weekly*, 1942, 5 Oct. 1927. Bill & the Toppers.
BK	*The Lady of Little Hell.* Bill & the Toppers.

No. 4	Nov. 1964 THE QUEEN OF SHEBA'S BELT (I suppose there's nothing more to be said . . .)
BK	*The Ghost of Down Hill.* The Queen of Sheba's Belt.
MG	*Grand Magazine*, Vol. 21, Mar. to June 1914. The Queen of Sheba's Belt.

No. 5	Dec. 1964 PLANETOID 127 (Chap West, who was never . . .)
MG	*Mechanical Boy*, 1–8, 4 Sept. to 23 Oct. 1924. Planetoid 127.
BK	*Planetoid* 127. Planetoid 127.

No. 6   Jan. 1965 THE HAUNTED ROOM (Dr. John Graham's study was a . . .)

THE BOSS OF THE BIG FOUR (To all outward appearance . . .)

BK   *The Big Four*. The Big Four Syndicate & the Man Who Smashed it.

No. 7   Feb. 1965 THE FALL OF SENTIMENTAL SIMPSON (According to certain signs . . .)

BK   *Forty Eight Short Stories*. Sentimental Simpson

BK   *The Cat Burglar*. Sentimental Simpson.

BK   *The Cat Burglar*. Sentimental Simpson.

MG   *Happy Magazine*, No. 1, June 1922. The Sentimental Crook.

No. 8   Mar. 1965 THE CLUE OF MONDAYS SETTLING (It did not seem possible to . . .)

BK   *Forty Eight Short Stories*. The Clue of Mondays Settling.

BK   *The Cat Burglar*. The Clue of Mondays Settling.

BK   *Fifty Masterpiece of Mystery*. The Clue of Mondays Settling.

No. 9   Apr. 1965 CIRCUMSTANTIAL EVIDENCE (Colonel Chartres Dane lingered . . .)

BK   *Forty Eight Short Stories*. Circumstantial Evidence.

BK   *Circumstantial Evidence*. Circumstantial Evidence.

BK   *Black Cap*. Circumstantial Evidence.

MG   *Strand Magazine*, Aug. 1922. Circumstantial Evidence.

No. 10   May 1965 THE SUBURBAN LOTHARIO (True Crime) (It is a natural thing . . .)

No. 11   June 1965 THE MAN WHO NEVER LOST (The man in the grey . . .)

BK	*Forty Eight Short Stories*. The Man Who Never Lost.
BK	*The Little Green Man*. The Man Who Never Lost.
MG	*Thriller*, 290, 25 Aug. 1934. The Man Who Never Lost.
MG	*Town Topics*, 383/4, 27 Dec. 1919 to 3 Jan. 1920. The Man Who Never Lost.

No. 12   July 1965 MUTATION IN PEARLS (Lord Heppleworth looked over his . . .)

BK   *The Big Four*. The Heppleworth Pearls.

No. 13   Aug. 1965 THE SIRIUS MAN (The Orator was not in his most . . .)

BK   *The Orator*. The Sirius Man.

MG   *Topical Times*, 493, 27 Apr. 1929. The Sirius Man.

MG   *Pall Mall Magazine*, Vol. 1, No. 9, Jan. 1928. The Sirius Man.

No. 14   Sept. 1965 THE GUY FROM MEMPHIS (There was a society of men and women . . .)

BK   *The Orator*. The Guy from Memphis.

MG   *Topical Times*, 496, 18 May 1929. The Guy from Memphis.

MG   *Pall Mall Magazine*, Vol. 1, No. 13, May 1928. The Guy from Memphis.

No. 15   Oct. 1965 DUO IN BLUE

1. CHANGE (One of the rummiest fellers . . .)

BK   *The Undisclosed Client*. Change.
      The Lady Called Nita. Mr. Sigee's Relations.

MG   *Ideas*, 209, 17 Mar. 1909. Change.

2. THE SENTIMENTAL BURGLAR (I was wondering in my mind . . .)

BK   *The Undisclosed Client*. The Sentimental Burglar.

MG   *Ideas*, 208, 10 Mar. 1909. The Sentimental Burglar.

No. 16.   Nov. 1965 THE REMARKABLE MR. REEDER (There was a quietude and sedateness . . .)

BK   *The Mind of Mr. J. G. Reeder*. The Troupe.

MG   *Thriller*, 307, 22 Dec. 1934. The Remarkable Mr. Reeder.

MG   *Grand Magazine*, Vol. 46, Sept. 1924 to Feb. 1925. A Place on the River.

No. 17.   Dec. 1965 ⎫

No. 18.   Jan. 1966 ⎬ Angel Esquire.

No. 19.   Feb. 1966 ⎪

No. 20.   Mar. 1966 ⎭

BK   *Angel Esquire.*

MG   *Ideas*, 149–157, 25 Jan. to 18 Mar. 1908. Angel Esquire.

No. 21.   Apr. 1966 A JUDGE OF RACING (The Honourable Mr. Justice Bellfont . . .)

BK   *More Educated Evans*. A Judge of Racing.

No. 22.   May 1966 CODE NO. 2 (The secret service never . . .)

BK   *Forty Eight Short Stories*. Code No. 2.

BK   *The Little Green Man*. Code No. 2.

MG   *Strand Magazine* Vol? Jan. to June 1916. Code. No. 2.

No. 23.   June 1966 THE KILLER OF LIOSKI (In Carolina in the Transvaal . . .)

BK   *Forty Eight Short Stories*. The Greek Poropulos.

BK   *The Governor of Chi-Foo*. The Greek Poropulos.

MG   *Weekly Tale Teller*, 81, 19 Nov. 1910. The Greek Poropulos.

BK   *The Thief in the Night* (Digit). The Greek Poropulos.

No. 24.	July 1966 THE BURGLARY AT GOODWOOD (Bob Brewer, temporary chief of . . .)
BK	*The Big Four*. The Burglary at Goodwood.
No. 25.	Aug. 1966 THEY WALKED AWAY (There are eight million people . . .)
BK	*The Mind of Mr. J. G. Reeder*. The Investors.
MG	*Thriller*, 294, 22 Sept 1934. The Investors.
MG	*Grand Magazine*, Vol. 47, Mar to Aug. 1925. The Investors.
MG	*Saint Magazine* (Br.), Aug. 1956. The Disappearing Investors.
No. 26.	Sept. 1966 BLACKMAIL WITH ROSES (Gather ye rosebuds while ye may . . .) Previously unpublished as per E. W. Ltd.
No. 27.	Oct. 1966 SHEER MELODRAMA (It was Mr. Reeder who planned . . .)
BK	*The Mind of Mr. J. G. Reeder*. Sheer Melodrama.
MG	*Thriller*, 289, 18 Aug. 1934. Sheer Melodrama.
MG	*Grand Magazine*, Vol. 47. Mar. to Aug. 1925. The Man from the East.
No. 28.	Nov. 1966 THE DEVIL DOCTOR (George Rewen had a weakness . . .)
BK	*The Last Adventure*. The Devil Doctor.
No. 29.	Dec. 1966 THE CHRISTMAS CUP (Colonel Desboro was an easy . . .)
BK	*Forty Eight Short Stories*. The Christmas Cup.
BK	*Fighting Snub Reilly*. The Christmas Cup.
BK	*The Undisclosed Client*. The Christmas Cup.
MG	*Windsor Magazine*, Vol. 63, Dec. 1925 to May 1926. The Christmas Cup.
MG	*Royal Magazine*, 1929. He Who Could Ride.
No. 30.	Jan 1967 THE PRISON BREAKERS (It was the sort of thing . . .)
BK	*Forty Eight Short Stories*. The Prison Breakers.

BK	*The Prison Breakers*. The Prison Breakers.
MG	*Thriller*, 288, 11 Aug. 1934. The Prison Breakers.
No. 31.	Feb. 1967 RICOCHET IN PEARLS (There was a sound of revelry . . .) Previously unpublished as per E. W. Ltd.
No. 32.	Mar. 1967 WARM & DRY (I went down to see Superintendent Minter . . .)
BK	*The Black*. Warm & Dry (Digit Edition only).
No. 33.	Apr. 1967 THE WIMBLEDON VAMPIRE (The Gentle Tressa was remarkable . . .)
N	*The People*, 4 May 24. The Vampire of Wembley.
No. 34.	May 1967 THE GIRL WHO WON AT EPSOM (When Alicia Penton entered the . . .)
N	*The People*, 27 Apr. 1924. The Girl Who Won at Epsom.
No. 35.	June 1967 THE LIGHT IN E FLAT (Some men have aversion to cats . . .) Previously unpublished as per E. W. Ltd.

Evening Standard

	6 June 1934 WHITE STOCKING
BK	*The Cat Burglar*. White Stocking.
BK	*Forty Eight Short Stories*. White Stocking.
MG	*Grand Magazine*, Vol. 41, Mar. to Aug. 1922. White Stocking.
MG	*Thriller*, 312, 26 Jan. 1935. White Stocking.
	5 Aug. 1935 THE MIND READERS
BK	*The Orator*. The Mind Readers.
MG	*Topical Times*, 488. 22 Mar. 1929. The Mind Readers.
MG	*Pall Mall Magazine*, Vol. 1, No. 6, Oct. 1927. The Mind Readers.

BK	*Fifty Famous Detectives of Fiction*. The Mind Readers.
34925	3 Aug. 1936 THE STEALER OF MARBLE
BK	*The Mind of Mr. J. G. Reeder*. The Stealer of Marble.
MG	*Grand Magazine*, Vol. 46, Sept. 1924 to Feb. 1925. The Telephone Box.
35365	4 Jan. 1938 MIXING IT (Every man has his sycophants . . .)
BK	*More Educated Evans*. Mixing It.

Grand Magazine (Newnes)

Vol. 6	1908 A BALLOON & A SCEPTIC (On the night of the 16th December 1917 . . .)
Vol. 7	July 1908 ALBERT SIGEE'S REMINISCENCES (It is certainly not my place . . .)
Vol. 21	Mar. to June 1914 THE QUEEN OF SHEBA'S BELT (I suppose there's nothing more to be said . . .)
BK	*The Ghost of Downhill*. The Queen of Sheba's Belt.
MG	*E.W.M.M.* (Br.), No. 4, Nov. 1964. The Queen of Sheba's Belt.
Vol. 28	Jan. to Oct. 1916 THE CLUE OF THE TWISTED CANDLE.
Vol. 29	Nov. 1916 to Feb. 1917) THE CLUE OF THE TWISTED CANDLE (The 4.15 from Victoria . . .)
BK	*The Clue of the Twisted Candle*.

The Strange Lapses of Larry Lomans

Vol. 31	July to Oct. 1917 1. THE CRIME TRUST (Sir George Grayburn leant back . . .) 2. THE AFFAIR OF THE STOKEHOLE (Larry Loman of the criminal . . .)

Vol. 32   Nov. 1917 to Feb. 1918 3. THE HERZEIMER WEDDING PRESENT (The name of Lewis Herzeimer . . .)

4. LORD EXENHAM CREATES A SENSATION (The bombshell which Lord Exenham . . .)

Vol. 34   Sept. 1918 to Feb. 1919 THE U BEAST (I've been sitting here for four . . .)

Vol. 37   Mar. to Aug. 1920 THE MAN IN THE GOLF HUT (He walked down the stairs . . .)

BK   *Fighting Snub Reilly*. The Man in the Golf Hut.

BK   *Forty Eight Short Stories*. The Man in the Golf Hut.

Vol. 39   Mar. to Aug. 1921 THE DAUGHTERS OF THE NIGHT (Jim Bartholomew, booted and spurred . . .)

BK   *The Daughters of the Night*.

Vol. 40   Sept. 1921 to Feb. 1922 TAM'S AIR TAXI (Beneath them was a dull . . .)

BK   *Killer Kay*. The Air Taxi.

THE PEDLAR IN THE MASK (Arthur Confort was a young man . . .)

BK   *The Last Adventure*. The Pedlar in the Mask.

Vol. 40   Sept. 1921 to Feb. 1922 THE GAMBLING GIRL.

Vol. 41   Mar. to Aug. 1922 THE GAMBLING GIRL (To write the true story of . . .)

Vol. 41   Mar. to Aug. 1922 WHITE STOCKING (John Trevor was not a jealous man . . .)

BK   *The Cat Burglar*. White Stocking.

BK   *Forty Eight Short Stories*. White Stocking.

MG   *Thriller*, 312, 26 Jan. 1935. White Stocking.

N   *Evening Standard*, 6 Jan. 1934. White Stocking.

SANCTUARY (Despite the gloomy prediction of . . .)

	Lords of the Nimble Pack (In the old days . . .)
BK	*The Steward*. The Barons of the Nimble Pack.
Vol. 44	Sept. 1923 to Feb. 1924 The Timid Admirer (Mirabelle Stoll read the morning paper . . .)
BK	*For Information Received*. The Timid Admirer.
Vol. 45	Mar. to Aug. 1924 The Ghost of John Holling (There are things about . . .)
BK	*The Steward*. The Ghost of John Holling.
	Diana the Disturbing (She is an orphan, said Mr. Collings . . .)
BK	*Double Dan.*
MG	*Happy Magazine*, 62–68, July 1927 to Jan. 1928. Double Dan.
Vol. 46.	Sept. 1924 to Feb. 1925 A Deed of Gift (Lord Derrymere read the paragraph . . .)
BK	*The Lady of Little Hell*. Fate & Mr. Hoke.

The Man Who Saw Evil

	1. The Strange Case of the Night Watchman (The day Mr. Reeder arrived . . .)
BK	*Fifty Famous Detectives of* Fiction. The Poetical Policeman.
BK	*The Mind of Mr. J. G. Reeder*. The Poetical Policeman.
MG	*Thriller*, 304, 1 Dec. 1934. The Poet Policeman.
MG	*Saint Magazine* (Br.), Sept. 1955. The Poetical Policeman.
	2. The Treasure Hunt (There is a tradition in criminal . . .)
BK	*The Mind of Mr. J. G. Reeder*. The Treasure Hunt.
MG	*Thriller*, 287, 4 Aug. 1934. The Treasure Hunt.
MG	*Saint Magazine* (Br.), Jan. 1956. The Treasure of Mr. Reeder.

3. A P<small>LACE ON THE</small> R<small>IVER</small> (There is a quietude and sedateness . . .)

BK   *The Mind of Mr. J. G. Reeder*. The Troupe. Mr Reeder.

MG   *Thriller*, 307, 22 Dec. 1934. *The Remarkable* M<small>R</small> R<small>EEDER</small>

MG   *E.W.M.M.* (Br.), No. 16, Nov. 1965. The Remarkable Mr. Reeder.

4. T<small>HE</small> T<small>ELEPHONE</small> B<small>OX</small> (Margaret Belman's chiefest claim . . .)

BK   *The Mind of Mr. J. G. Reeder*. The Stealer of Marble.

N   *Evening Standard*, 3 Aug. 1936. The Stealer of Marble.

MG   *Grand Magazine*, Vol. 46, Sept. 1924 to Feb. 1925. A Place on the River.

Vol. 47   Mar. to Aug. 1925.

5. T<small>HE</small> M<small>AN FROM THE</small> E<small>AST</small> (It was Mr. Reeder who planned . . .)

BK   *The Mind of Mr. J. G. Reeder*. Sheer Melodrama.

MG   *Thriller*, 289, 18 Aug. 1934. Sheer Melodrama.

MG   *E.W.M.M.* (Br.), No. 27. Oct. 1966. Sheer Melodrama.

6. T<small>HE</small> D<small>ANGEROUS</small> R<small>EPTILE</small> (The spirit of exploration . . .)

BK   *The Mind of Mr. J. G. Reeder*. The Green Mamba.

MG   *Thriller*, 292, 8 Sept. 1934. The Green Mamba.

7. T<small>HE</small> W<small>EAK</small> S<small>POT</small> (In the days of Mr. Reeder's youth . . .)

BK   *The Mind of Mr J. G. Reeder*. The Strange Case.

8. T<small>HE</small> I<small>NVESTORS</small> (There are seven million people . . .)

BK   *The Mind of Mr. J. G. Reeder*. The Investors.

MG   *Thriller*, 294, 22 Sept. 1934. The Investors.

MG	*E.W.M.M.* (Br.), No. 25, Aug. 1966. They Walked Away.
MG	*Saint Magazine* (Br.) Aug. 1956. The Disappearing Investors.
	BONES & THE MAGIC MUSIC (The Soldiers of the old King who . . .)
BK	*Sanders*. The Clean Sweeper.
Vol. 48	Sept. 1925 to Feb. 1926.
	BONES & THE QUALIFIED NURSE (The spectacle of a white man . . .)
BK	*Sanders*. The Very Good Man.
	BONES PROPOSES (Doran Campbell-Cairns was very kind . . .)
BK	*Sanders*. The Ball Game.
	THE CAPTURE OF BONES (When Lieutenant Tibbetts had a great educational . . .)
BK	*Sanders*. The Sweet Singer.
	THE VINDICATION OF BONES (Mr. Commissioner Sanders' launch . . .)
	BONES & THE GOLD SEEKER (Beyond the forest of happy dreams . . .)
BK	*Sanders*. The Man Who Hated Sheffield.
	BONES & THE GHOST MEN (At rare intervals, once in a . . .)
BK	*Sanders*. The Wise Man.
Vol. 49	Mar. to Aug. 1926.
	BONES & THE SAINT (From time to time there passed . . .)
BK	*Sanders*. The Saint.
	THE MAGIC OF FEAR (There was an under-Secretary . . .)
	THE LITTLE BARONESS (When you're twenty one . . .)
BK	*The Steward*. The Little Baroness.
MG	*Saint Magazine* (Br.), May 1964. The Little Baroness.

	DECLARED TO WIN (John Petworth came out of the army . . .)
BK	*The Lady of Little Hell*. Declared to Win.
	BONES FALLS IN LOVE (The two splendid things . . .)
BK	*Again Sanders*. The Splendid Things.

Happy Magazine (Newnes)

No. 1.	June 1922 THE SENTIMENTAL CROOK (According to certain signs . . .)
BK	*The Cat Burglar*. Sentimental Simpson.
BK	*Forty Eight Short Stories*. Sentimental Simpson.
MG	*E.W.M.M.* (Br.) No. 7, Feb. 1965. The Fall of Sentimental Simpson.
No. 8.	Jan. 1923 A ROMANCE IN BROWN (Romance . . .! Yes I suppose . . .)
BK	*Fighting Snub Reilly*. A Romance in Brown.
BK	*Forty Eight Short Stories*. A Romance in Brown.
No. 12.	May 1923 A MAN OF HIS WORD (Jake Feld saw Long Sam . . .)
BK	*The Last Adventure*. The Trimming of Sam.
Nos. 62–68.	July 1927 to Jan. 1928 DOUBLE DAN
BK	*Double Dan*.
MG	*Grand Magazine*, Vol. 45, Mar. to Aug. 1924. Diana the Disturbing.

Harmsworth's All-Story Magazine

	Aug. 1927 THE SILVER CHARM (Angel, Esquire, has a little office . . .)
MG	*Story Teller*, June 1910. The Silver Charm.
BK	*Woman from the East*. The Silver Charm.

Ideas (Hultons)

| 1 | 30 Jan. 1905 'TOMMY' (Article) |

135	17 Oct. 1907 THE RETURN OF SMITHY
136	24 Oct. 1907 SMITHY'S BAND OF HEROES
BK	*Nobby*. The Heroes.
137	31 Oct. 1907 SMITHY & THE FIGHTING AN-CHESTERS
BK	*Nobby*. The Fighting Anchesters.
138	7 Nov. 1907 SMITHY ON FINANCE
BK	*Nobby*. On Finance.
139	14 Nov. 1907 SMITHY ON PROMOTION
BK	*Nobby*. On Promotion.
140	21 Nov. 1907 SMITHY—AMBASSADOR
BK	*Nobby*. Smith—Ambassador.
141	28 Nov. 1907 NOBBY'S DOUBLE
BK	*Nobby*. Nobby's Double.
142	5 Dec. 1907 'SMITHY' ON AUTHORSHIP
BK	*Nobby*. Authorship.
143	12 Dec. 1907 'SMITHY' ADVOCATES 'RAGGING'
144	19 Dec. 1907 'SMITHY' IN TEARS
145	26 Dec. 1907 'SMITHY' ON ADVERTISING
BK	*Nobby*. On Advertising.
146	2 Jan. 1908 'SMITHY' ON HOGMANAY
BK	*Nobby*. Hogmanay.
147	9 Jan. 1908 'SMITHY' AS A LAST LINER
148	16 Jan. 1908 SMITHY'S DESCENT UPON LONDON
149	25 Jan. 1908 'SMITHY' TIRES OF WEALTH
149–157	25 Jan. 1908 to 18 Mar. 1908 ANGEL ESQUIRE (Mr. William Spedding, of the firm . . .)
BK	*Angel Esquire*
150	1 Feb. 1908 'SMITHY' & THE BAA LAMB
BK	*Nobby*. The Baa-Lamb.
151	8 Feb. 1908 'SMITHY' GOES RACING AND 'MAKES A BIT'

190	4 Nov. 1908 13. THE FOOTBALL MATCH
BK	*Smithy Abroad.* The Football Match.
191	11 Nov. 1908 14. THATCHER'S BROTHER
BK	*Smithy Abroad.* Thatcher's Brother.
192	18 Nov. 1908 15. THE INVENTION CRAZE
BK	*Smithy Abroad.* The Invention Craze.
193	25 Nov. 1908 16. MARSHY, DETECTIVE
BK	*Smithy Abroad.* Marshy, Detective.
194	2 Dec. 1908 17. THE GHOST OF THE BROOK
BK	*Smithy Abroad.* The Ghost of the Brook.
195	9 Dec. 1908 18. SMITHY ON HUMOUR
BK	*Smithy Abroad.* Smithy on Humour.
196	16 Dec. 1908 19. PIKEY'S LUCK
BK	*Smithy Abroad.* Pikey's Luck.
197	23 Dec. 1908 20. THE BUGLERS
BK	*Smithy Abroad.* The Buglers.
198	30 Dec. 1908 21. HONOUR
BK	*Smithy Abroad.* Honour.
199	6 Jan. 1909 22. SACRIFICE
BK	*Smithy Abroad.* Sacrifice.
200	13 Jan. 1909 23. A SUPRESSED BOOK
BK	*Smithy Abroad.* A Supressed Book.
201	21 Jan. 1909 24. A SOLDIER & A MAN
BK	*Smithy Abroad:* A Soldier & a Man.

P.C. Lee of 'D'

202	27 Jan. 1909 1. MR. SIMMON'S PROFESSION (The magistrate looked over . . .)
BK	*The Undisclosed Client.* Mr. Simmon's Profession.
MG	*Ideas*, 1239, 8 Dec. 1928. Mr. Simmon's Profession.
203	3 Feb. 1909 2. A MAN OF NOTE (Once I hinted delicately to . . .)

Ideas

211	31 Mar. 1909 10. CONTEMPT (Six years ago I sat in the . . .)
BK	*The Undisclosed Client*: Contempt.
MG	*Ideas*, 1247, 2 Feb. 1929. When the Jury Came to Blows.
212	7 Apr. 1909 11. CONFIDENCE (A Policeman, said P.C. Lee . . .)
MG	*Ideas*, 1245, 19 Jan. 1929. Chicago Harry Meets his Match.
213	14 Apr. 1909 12. FIRELESS TELEGRAPHY (Talkin' about foreigners . . .)
214	21 Mar. 1909 13. THE GENERAL PRACTITIONER (Genius, said P.C. Lee . . .)
MG	*Ideas* 1242, 29 Dec. 1928. The Crime Specialist's Mistake.
215	28 Apr. 1909 14. THE SNATCHERS (When people talk . . .)
216	5 May 1909 15. THE GOLD MINE (Mysteries, such as you . . .)
217	12 May 1909 16. MOULDY THE SCRIVENER (I sat down . . .)
218	19 May 1909 17. MRS. FLINDIN'S LODGER P.C. Lee has . . .)
219	26 May 1909 18. THE DERBY FAVOURITE (Likely enough . . .)
220	2 June 1909 19. THE STORY OF A GREAT CROSS EXAMINATION ('Lawyers', said P.C. Lee . . .)
221	9 June 1909 20. TANKS (Roughs there are as is well . . .)
MG	*Ideas*, 1241, 22 Dec. 1928. An Arrest that Made the Sergeant Laugh.
222	16 June 1909 21. THE SILENCE OF P.C. HIRLEY (The art of being a policeman . . .)
MG	*Ideas*, 1244, 12 Jan. 1929. The Secret of the Silent Policeman.

The 'Makings-Up' of Nobby Clark

Clarence Clark M.P.

The Return of Smithy

Translated from the Russian of Paula Vladimir).

426	10 May 1913 HOW I WROTE A PLAY (I wrote a play . . .)
435	12 July 1913 A MODERN PAGLIACCI (The other comedian was holding . . .) 'One page)
442	30 Aug. 1913 IS YOUR NAME BILL! (article)
765–770	5 Nov. 1919 to 10 Dec. 1919 BRANDED MILLIONS (Wulbur Smith read the letter . . .)
BK	*The Golden Hades*
1037–1049	17 Jan. 1925 to 11 Apr. 1925 MY LADY SATAN (The hush of the Court . . .)
BK	*The Angel of Terror*
1091–1095	30 Jan. 1926 to 27 Feb. 1926 BY WHOSE HAND (With such patience as a young and well . . .)
BK	Abridged version of: *Flat 2*
1217	7 July 1928 WHILE THE PASSENGERS SLEPT (The dismal clang of the bell . . .)
1239	8 Dec. 1928 MR. SIMMONS' PROFESSION (The magistrate looked over . . .)
BK	*The Undisclosed Client.* Mr. Simmons' Profession.
MG	*Ideas*, 202, 27 Jan. 1909. Mr Simmons' Profession.
1240	15 Dec. 1928 JEWEYS LAGGIN (People get queer notions . . .)
BK	*The Undisclosed Client.* For Jeweys Laggin.
MG	*Ideas*, 204, 10 Feb. 1909. For Jeweys Laggin.
1241	22 Dec. 1928 AN ARREST THAT MADE THE SERGEANT LAUGH (Roughs there are, as is well . . .)
MG	*Ideas*, 221, 9 June 1909. Tanks.

1242	29 Dec. 1928 THE CRIME SPECIALIST'S MISTAKE ('Genius,' said P,C.Lee . . .)
MG	*Ideas*, 214, 21 Apr. 1909. The General Practitioner.
1243	5 Jan. 1929 THE COURTSHIP OF SERGEANT 'RUN-A-MILE' (The Police Force said P.C. Lee . . .)
BK	*The Undisclosed Client* Sergeant Run-a-Mile.
MG	*Ideas*, 207, 3 Mar. 1909. Sergeant Run-a-Mile.
1244	12 Jan. 1929 THE SECRET OF THE SILENT POLICEMAN (The art of being a policeman . . .)
MG	*Ideas*, 222, 16 June 1909. The Silence of P.C. Hirley.
1245	19 Jan. 1929 CHICAGO HARRY MEETS HIS MATCH (A Policeman said P.C. Lee . . .)
MG	*Ideas*, 212 7 Apr. 1909. Confidence.
1246	26 Jan. 1929 THE INSPECTOR GETS A BRAINWAVE (There was a minister of France . . .)
MG	*Ideas*, 210, 24 Mar. 1909. A Case for Angel Esquire.
1247	2 Feb. 1929 WHEN THE JURY CAME TO BLOWS (Sometime ago I sat . . .)
BK	*The Undisclosed Client*. Contempt.
MG	*Ideas*, 211, 31 Mar. 1909. Contempt.
1248	9 Feb. 1929 THE MAN WHO SHOT THE FAVOURITE (There always will be . . .)

John Bull (Odhams)

| 830 | 29 Apr. 1922 THE REAL DOPE CLUBS (article) |

Sportingalities (articles)

841	15 July 1922 1. LORD DERBY
842	22 July 1922 2. SOLOMON B. JOEL
843	29 July 1922 3. SIR SAMUEL SCOTT
844	5 Aug. 1922 4. MR. ALEC TAYLOR

845	12 Aug. 1922 5. BERT JONES
846	19 Aug. 1922 6. LORD LONSDALE
847	26 Aug. 1922 7. BOMBADIER WELLS
848	2 Sept. 1922 8. GEORGE CARPENTIER
849	9 Sept. 1922 9. LORD ASTOR
850	16 Sept. 1922 10. LORD CARNARVON
872–888	17 Feb. 1923 to 9 June 1923 MY CONFESSIONS OF TURF SWINDLING BY P.C. (PAT) BARRIE ghosted by Edgar Wallace.
949	9 Aug. 1924 ARE MURDER TRIALS FAIR? (article)
969	27 Dec. 1924 'CAT' CRIMES—THE TRUTH!
1186	2 Feb. 1929 HOW I DISCOVERED A MURDER (article)
1196	18 May 1929 MY HEART-TO-HEART TALK ON THE 'TALKIES' (article)
1201	22 June 1929 MYSTERIES OF ASCOT (article)
1206	27 July 1929 RACING STABLE SECRETS (article)
1247	10 May 1930 WORSE THAN THE WORST CRIMINAL (article)
1253	21 June 1930 THE PLAGUE OF MURDERS (article)
1306	27 June 1931 WHAT HAS HAPPENED TO EDGAR WALLACE'S GHOST? (article)

John Bull Specials

Xmas Annual 1922	SIR JOHN'S XMAS DAY (Christmas Day Hum—?)
Xmas Annual 1926	'STUFFING' (There are several people concerned . . .)

Summer Annual 1927	'THE PICK UP' (It was the day before . . .)
BK	*The Cat Burglar*. The Pick Up.
BK	*Forty Eight Short Stories*. The Pick Up.
Xmas Annual 1927	THE SHARE PUSHER (The man whom Raymond Poiccart . . .)
BK	*Again the Three*. The Share Pusher.

London Calling (Amalgamated Press)
Golden Rules for Racing (articles)

1	3 Mar. 1928 CATCH YOUR HORSE
2	10 Mar. 1928 NEXT CATCH YOUR JOCKEY
3	17 Mar. 1928 NEXT FIND A TRAINER
4	24 Mar. 1928 NEXT FIND A BOOKIE
5	31 Mar. 1928 EDGAR WALLACE ON THE BIG DOUBLE
6	7 Apr. 1928 EDGAR WALLACE ON DOUBLE HORSES TO FOLLOW
31	29 Sept. 1928 EDGAR WALLACE ON THE POLICE (article)
42	8 Dec. 1928 THE WALLACEUM BY HANNEN SWAFFER

London Mail

13 Mar. 1926 IMPERTINENT INTERVIEWS No. 4, Edgar Wallace, 'The Human Machine'.

Merry Magazine

No. 8, Feb. 1925 THE FEARFUL FOUR. (A man who calls his unprotected . . .)

BK   *Mrs. William Jones and Bill*. The Society of Bright Young People.

No. 13, July 1925 THE WILL AND THE WONT. (People only make such wills . . .)

BK   *The Last Adventure*. The Will and the Way.

Mechanical Boy (Percival Marshall & Co.)

Nos. 1–8   4 Sept. to 23 Oct. 1924 PLANETOID 127
BK   *Planetoid* 127.
MG   *E.W.M.M.* (Br.), No. 5, Dec. 1964. Planetoid 127.

Pall Mall Magazine

*May 1909 THE BARFORD SNAKE (Every railwayman knows the Barford Snake . . .)
Oct. 1909. THE FOREST OF HAPPY THOUGHTS (Bailman made things snug for the night . . .)

Nash's Illustrated Weekly (Hutchinson)

19   17 Jan. 1920 A GIRL AMONG THIEVES (In the old days the Howarths . . .)
BK   *Lady Called Nita:* Her Father's Daughter.
MG   20 *Story Magazine*, Oct. 1929. Her Father's Daughter.

20   24 Jan. 1920 THE MAN WHO GOT AWAY (Between F.O.I. and the office of the interior . . .)

Pall Mall Magazine (new series)
Vol. 1.

4   Aug. 1927 THE ORATOR (They called Chief Inspector Rater . . .)
MG   *Topical Times*, 487, 16 Mar. 1929. The Poisoned Cup.
BK   *The Orator*. The Orator.

*Edgar Wallace stated in his autobiography that this was his first story published in a London magazine.

5	Sept. 1927 THE OLD LADY WHO CHANGED HER MIND (Mr. Rater never took a job . . .)
MG	*Topical Times*, 489, 30 Mar. 1929. The Old Lady who Changed her Mind.
BK	*The Orator*: The Old Lady who Changed her Mind.
6	Oct. 1927 THE MIND READER (There is no police force in the world . . .)
MG	*Topical Times*, 488, 23 Mar. 1929. The Mind Readers.
BK	*The Orator*. The Mind Readers.
N	*Evening Standard*, 5 Aug. 1935. The Mind Readers.
BK	*Fifty Famous Detectives of Fiction*. The Mind Readers.
7	Nov. 1927 A BANK & A SECRETARY (The Orator knew the London & Southern . . .)
MG	*Topical Times*, 491, 13 Apr. 1929. A Bank & a Secretary.
BK	*The Orator*. A Bank & a Secretary.
8	Dec. 1927 THE SUNNINGDALE MURDER (There was a certain assistant . . .)
MG	*Topical Times*, 490, 6 Apr. 1929. The Sunningdale Murder.
BK	*The Orator*. The Sunningdale Murder.
9	Jan. 1928 THE SIRIUS MAN (The Orator was not in his most. . .)
MG	*Topical Times*, 493, 27 Apr. 1929. The Sirius Man.
	The Orator. The Sirius Man.
MG	*E.W.M.M.* (Br.), No. 13, Aug. 1965. The Sirius Man.
10	Feb. 1928 THE MAN NEXT DOOR (When Mr. Giles walked into the . . .)

MG	*Topical Times*, 492, 20 Apr. 1929. The Man Next Door.
BK	*The Orator*. The Man Next Door.

11	Mar. 1928 THE FIRST NIGHT (Inspector Rater very seldom went . . .)
MG	*Topical Timer*, 495, 11 May 1929. The Case of Caper Vane.
BK	*The Orator*. The Case of Freddie Vane.

12	Apr. 1928 THE COUPER BUCKLE (Inspector Rater had a friend . . .)
MG	*Topical Times*, 494, 4 May. 1929. The Couper Buckle.
BK	*The Orator*. The Couper Buckle.

13	May 1928 THE GUY FROM MEMPHIS (There was a society of men and women . . .)
MG	*Topical Times*, 496, 18 May 1929. The Guy from Memphis.
BK	*The Orator*. The Guy from Memphis.
MG	*E.W.M.M.* (Br.), No. 14, Sept. 1965. The Guy from Memphis.

14	June 1928 THE ORATOR'S DOWNFALL (The Orator was a man who had very . . .)
MG	*Topical Times*, 498, 1 June 1929. The Fall of Mr. Rater.
BK	*The Orator*. The Fall of Mr. Rater.

15	July 1928 THE DETECTIVE WHO TALKED (Let me say at first I was never . . .)
MG	*Topical Times*, 497, 25 May 1929. The Detective who Talked.
BK	*The Orator*. The Detective who Talked.

	Dec. 1928 THE LEFT PASS (There was a lady artist . . .)
BK	*The Steward*. The Left Pass.

New London Magazine (Amalgamated Press)

> Dec. 1930 HOUSEKEEPING FOR A GENIUS (article) by Mrs. Edgar Wallace.
> Supplement with photograph of Edgar Wallace's home at Bourne End.

News of the World

3868–3882	9 Dec. 1917 to 17 Mar. 1918 PATRIA (Last of the Fighting Channings) (Captain Donald of the United States . . .) From the film by Pathe Freres Cinema Ltd.
3918–3933	24 Nov. 1919 to 9 Mar. 1919 THE GREEN TERROR (I don't know whether there's a law . . .
BK	*The Green Rust*
4090–4106	19 Mar. 1922 to 9 July 1922 THE FLYING FIFTY-FIVE (Stella Barrington came through . . .)
BK	*The Flying Fifty-Five*
4209–4220	29 June to 14 Sept. 1924 THE DIAMOND MEN (The fog which was later to descend . . .)
BK	*The Face in the Night*
4302–4308	11 Apr. 1926 to 23 May 1926 THE LIFE STORY OF EDGAR WALLACE
4373–4384	21 Aug. 1927 to 6 Nov. 1927 THE TWISTER (In the summer of nineteen-twenty something . . .)
BK	*The Twister*
4479–4489	1 Sept 1929 to 10 Nov. 1929 THE GREEN RIBBON (Walking up Lower Regent Street . . .)
BK	*The Green Ribbon*

The New Strand (The New Strand Co.)

4	Mar. 1962 1. THE DEEMING MURDERS
5	Apr. 1962 2. SEDDON
6	May 1962 3. DOUGAL
7	June 1962 4. BENNETT

Novel Magazine

2–4: rewritten reprints from FAMOUS CRIMES OF MODERN TIMES. All true crime and were stated to be previously unpublished.

Novel Magazine

Feb. 1912 THE EDUCATION OF THE KING (Mr. Commissioner Sanders had graduated . . .)

BK   *Sanders of the River*. The Education of the King.

MG   *Weekly Tale Teller* 38, 22 Jan. 1910. The Exploiter; 43, 26 Feb. 1019. The Education of King Peter.

Oct. 1912 THE SEVENTH MAN—a complete story written by five authors, each author contributing one chapter: W. Holt White; Ruby M. Ayres; W. Harold Thomson; Daisy May Edgington; Edgar Wallace. Chapter 5 by Edgar Wallace.

LOST OR WON (It was not the horrible face . . .)

Dec. 1912 THE TALKATIVE BURGLAR (No sooner had the white fan . . .)

BK   *The Last Adventure*. The Talkative Burglar.

MG   *Pearsons Weekly*, 1957, 28 Jan 1928. The Talkative Burglar.

April 1913 A QUESTION OF HONOUR (People say that Bulfox was a fool . . .)

BK   *Forty Eight Short Stories*. Bulfox Asleep.

BK   *The Prison Breakers*. Bulfox Asleep.

MG   *Pearsons Weekly*, 1980, 7 July 1928. Bulfox Asleep.

MG   20 *Story Magazine*, Jan. 1931. Bulfox Asleep.

July 1914 HER BIRTHDAY (Redwood, of the firm of Redwood . . .)

MG   *Pearsons Weekly*, 1982, 21 July 1928. Two Rogues & a Girl.

Oct. 1914 CHUBB OF THE 'SLIPPER' (There was
no doubt about Chubb's gift . . .)

BK   *Forty Eight Short Stories*. Chubb of the
'Slipper'.

BK   *The Little Green Man*. Chubb of the 'Slipper'.

Clarence—Private

Dec. 1914 1. THE BIRTH OF THE SHARP-
SHOOTERS (Fate played a low trick . . .)

Jan. 1915 2. THE WOMAN OF MONS (Private
Clarence Cassidy, untouched . . .)

Feb. 1915 3. THE RETURN OF THE GREAT
UNWANTED (Private Clarence Cassidy was
doubtless . . .)

Mar. 1915 4. THE LOSING OF ORLANDO (The
Guns were Talking . . .)

Apr. 1915 5. THE GHOST OF NAPOLEON (Four
Brothers serving . . .)

May 1915 6. THE RED CHOCOLATE (As I have
before . . .)

June 1915 WHEN THE TSAR CAME (Peter
Petervitch lived in a little . . .)

Feb. 1916 WHEN THE ARMANIC SANK (Marjorie
Swain said her uncle . . .)

May 1916 BATTLE LEVEL (Dalberry came down
the Broad . . .)

The Fighting Scouts

Oct. 1918 1. THE GENTLEMEN FROM INDIANA
(Lieutenant Boxter was writing . . .)

BK   *The Fighting Scouts*. The Gentlemen from
Indiana.

Nov. 1918 2. THE DUKE'S MUSEUM (When
the Grand Duke . . .)

BK   *The Fighting Scouts*. The Duke's Museum.

Dec. 1918 3. THE KINDERGARTEN (The entry of the United States . . .)

BK   *The Fighting Scouts.* The Kindergarten.

Jan. 1919 4. THE WAGER OF RITTMEISTER VON HAARDEN (There is amongst the children . . .)

BK   *The Fighting Scouts.* The Wager of Rittmeister Von Haarden.

Feb. 1919 5. THE DEBUT OF WILLIAM BEST (There is a loneliness . . .)

BK   *The Fighting Scouts.* The Debut of William Best.

Mar. 1919 6. THE WOMAN IN THE STORY (Tam Walked to the door . . .)

BK   *The Fighting Scouts.* The Woman in the Story.

April 1919 7. THE CLOUD FISHERS (Are you going . . .)

BK   *The Fighting Scouts.* The Cloud Fishers.

May 1919 8. THE INFANT SAMUEL ('Tam', said Billy . . .)

BK   *The Fighting Scouts.* The Infant Samuel.

Wise Y. Symon

July 1919 1. THE DUCHESS (York Symon was by common . . .)

BK   *The Reporter.* The Reporter.

MG   *Pearsons Weekly*, 1961, 25 Feb. 1928. The Duchess.

Aug. 1919 2. THE CARETAKER IN CHARGE (A Police-reporter has many . . .)

Sept. 1919 3. THE MURDER OF BENNETT SANDMAN (Symon swung his pyjama'd legs . . .)

BK   *The Reporter.* The Murder of Bennett Sandman.

MG   *Pearsons Weekly*, 1959, 11 Feb. 1928. The Murder of Bennett Sandman.

      Oct. 1919. 4. THE WRITINGS OF MACONOCHIE HOE (That Wise Symon was a great . . .)
BK   *The Reporter*. The Writings of Maconochie Hoe.
MG   *Pearsons Weekly*, 1965, 24 Mar. 1928. The Writings of Maconochie Hoe.

      Nov. 1919 5. THE CRIME OF GAI JOI (Mr. York Symon did not attain . . .)
BK   *The Reporter*. The Crime of Gai Joi.
MG   *Pearsons Weekly*, 1967, 7 Apr. 1928. The Crime of Gai Joi.

      Dec. 1919 6. THE LETHBRIDGE ABDUCTION (Do you really want to know . . .)
BK   *The Reporter*. The Lethbridge Abduction.
MG   *Pearsons Weekly*, 1968, 14 Apr. 1928. The Lethbridge Abduction.

      Jan. 1920 7. THE SOCIAL CLUB SAFE DEPOSIT (Wise Y. Symon strolled into his . . .)
BK   *The Reporter*. The Safe Deposit at the Social Club.
MG   *Pearsons Weekly*, 1970, 28 Apr. 1928. The Social Club Safe Deposit.

      Feb. 1920 8. THE CASE OF CROOK BERESFORD (Ordinarily, women did not greatly . . .)
BK   *The Reporter*. The Case of Crook Beresford.
MG   *Pearsons Weekly*, 1972, 12 May 1928. The Case of Crook Beresford.

      Mar. 1920 9. THE CRIME EXPERT (Wise Y. Symon, the prince of crime reporters . . .)
BK   *The Reporter*. The Crime Expert.
MG   *Pearsons Weekly*, 1954, 7 Jan. 1928. The Crime Expert.

April 1920 10. THE LAST THROW OF CROOK BERESFORD (The editor sent for Wise Symon . . .)

BK   *The Reporter*. The Last Throw of Crook Beresford.

MG   *Pearsons Weekly*, 1974, 26 May 1928. The Last Throw of Crook Beresford.

June 1920 to at least Oct. 1920 THE WOMAN WITH THE RED HANDS (John Sands had infinite faith in his star . . .)

BK   *The Million Dollar Story*

July 1921 THE SPEED TEST (Miss Jane Ida Meach . . .)

MG   *Pearsons Weekly*, 1976, 9 June 1928. Jimmy's Speed Test.

The Law of the Four

Aug. 1921 1. THE MAN WHO WOULD NOT SPEAK (There was no sphere of human . . .)

BK   *The Law of the Four Just Men*. The Man who Would Not Speak.

MG   *Thriller*, 321, 30 Mar. 1935. The Man who Would Not Speak.

Sept. 1921 2. THE MAN WHO LOVED MUSIC (The most striking characteristics . . .)

BK   *The Law of the Four Just Men*. The Man who Loved Music.

MG   *Thriller*, 319, 16 Mar. 1935. The Man who Loved Music.

The Nerve of Tony Newton

Jan. 1923 THE GUEST OF THE MINNOWS (Tony Newton was strong in . . .)

BK   *The Brigand*. The Guest of the Minnows.

Feb. 1923 THE BURSTED ELECTION (Tony was neither ambitious nor . . .)

BK	*The Brigand.* The Bursted Election.
MG	*Thriller*, 357, 7 Dec. 1935. Vote for Tony Newton.
	March 1923 THE JOKER (Mr. Anthony Newton had enjoyed . . .)
BK	*The Brigand.* The Joker.
MG	*Thriller*, 358, 14 Dec. 1935. The Joke of a Lifetime.
	April 1923 CROOKED DEALINGS (Tony Newton was an opportunist . . .)
BK	*The Brigand.* The Graft.

Pan (Odhams)

	Vol. 7 No. 10 April 1922 A BUSINESS TRAINING (It was Winifred Laudermere who suggested . . .)
BK	*For Information Received* A Business Training.
	Vol. 7–Vol. 9 May 1922 to Jan. 1923 THE VALLEY OF GHOSTS
BK	*The Valley of Ghosts* Incorporated into *20th Century Story Magazine.*

Pearsons Magazine

June 1935 THE GENIUS THAT WAS FATHER by P. Wallace (with photographs of family).

Pearsons Weekly (C. Arthur Pearson)

1942	5 Oct. 1927 BILL & THE TOPPERS (There was a very clever detective . . .)
BK	*Lady of Little Hell.* Bill & the Topper.
MG	*E.W.M.M.* (Br.), No. 3, Oct. 1964. Bill of Scotland Yard.

1949	3 Dec. 1927 THE WEAKLING (Rex Madlon was a nice boy . . .)
BK	*The Governor of Chi-Foo*. The Weakling.
BK	*Forty Eight Short Stories*. The Weakling.
1954	7 Jan. 1928 THE CRIME EXPERT (Wise Y. Simon, the Prince of crime reporters . . .)
BK	*The Reporter*. The Crime Expert.
MG	*Novel Magazine*, March 1920. The Crime Expert.
1957	28 Jan. 1928 THE TALKATIVE BURGLAR (No sooner had the white fan . . .)
BK	*The Last Adventure*. The Talkative Burglar.
MG	*Novel Magazine* Dec. 1912. The Talkative Burglar.
1959	11 Feb. 1928 THE MURDER OF BENNETT SANDMAN (Symon swung his pyjama'd legs . . .)
BK	*The Reporter*. The Murder of Bennett Sandman.
MG	*Novel Magazine*, Sept. 1919. The Murder of Bennett Sandman.
1961	25 Feb. 1928 THE DUCHESS (York Symon was by common . . .)
BK	*The Reporter*. The Reporter.
MG	*Novel Magazine*, July 1919. The Duchess.
1965	24 Mar. 1928 THE WRITINGS OF MACONOCHIE HOE (That Wise Symon was a great . . .)
BK	*The Reporter*. The Writings of Maconochie Hoe.
MG	*Novel Magazine* Oct. 1919. The Writings of Maconochie Hoe.
1967	7 Apr. 1928 THE CRIME OF GAI JOI (Mr. York Symon did not attain . . .)
BK	*The Reporter*. The Crime of Gai Joi.
MG	*Novel Magazine*, Nov. 1919. The Crime of Gai Joi.

1968	14 Apr. 1928 THE LETHBRIDGE ABDUCTION (Do you really want to know . . .)
BK	*The Reporter*. The Lethbridge Abduction.
MG	*Novel Magazine*, Dec. 1919. The Lethbridge Abduction.
1970	28 Apr. 1928 THE SOCIAL CLUB SAFE DEPOSIT (Wise Y. Symon strolled into his . . .)
BK	*The Reporter*. The Safe Deposit at the Social Club.
MG	*Novel Magazine*, Jan. 1920. The Social Club Safe Deposit.
1972	12 May 1928 THE CASE OF CROOK BERESFORD (Ordinarily, women did not greatly . . .)
BK	*The Reporter*. The Case of Crook Beresford.
MG	*Novel Magazine*, Feb. 1920. The Case of Crook Beresford.
1974	26 May 1928 THE LAST THROW OF CROOK BERESFORD (The editor sent for Wise Symon . . .)
BK	*The Reporter*. The Last Throw of Crook Beresford.
MG	*Novel Magazine*, April 1920. The Last Throw of Crook Beresford.
1976	9 June 1928 JIMMY'S SPEED TEST (Miss Jane Ida Meach . . .)
MG	*Novel Magazine*, July 1921. The Speed Test.
1978	23 June 1928 JIMMY & THE DOUGHNUTS (Jimmy—otherwise Miss Jane . . .)
BK	*The Woman from the East*. Jimmy & the Doughnuts.
1980	7 July 1928 A QUESTION OF HONOUR (People say that Bulfox was a fool . . .)
MG	*Novel Magazine*, April 1913. A Question of Honour.
BK	*The Prison Breakers*. Bulfox Asleep.

BK	*Forty Eight Short Stories*. Bulfox Asleep.
MG	20 *Story Magazine*, Jan. 1931. Bulfox Asleep.
1982	21 July 1928 TWO ROGUES & GIRL (Redwood, of the firm of Redwood . . .)
MG	*Novel Magazine*, July 1914. Her Birthday.
1994–2014	13 Oct. 1928 to 2 Mar. 1929 THE INDIA-RUBBER MEN (In the mist of a foggy morning . . .)
BK	*The India Rubber Men*
2016	16 Mar. 1929 WHEN EDGAR WALLACE KID-NAPPED ME (article) by Patricia Wallace.
2022	27 Apr. 1929 EDGAR WALLACE DEFENDS (A reply to Lord Birkenhead who criticised an E. W. thriller)
2054	7 Dec. 1929 THE CUSTODY OF THE CHILD (There were times when Mrs. Harvey . . .)
BK	*The Lady of Little Hell*. The Custody of the Child.
2056	21 Dec. 1929 WITH EDGAR WALLACE IN AMERICA by Pat Wallace.
2064	15 Feb, 1930. FOR THE KING'S COMFORT (Mr. Benjamin Thanet was a . . .)
MG	*Wild West Weekly*, No. 7. 23 Apr. 1938. The King who chased Butterflies.
MG	*Royal Magazine*, Dec. 1921. The Trust in Princes.
2164	16 Jan. 1932 IS CHICAGO AS BAD AS IT'S FILMED ? (article).
2171	5 Mar. 1932 EDGAR WALLACE CHANGED MY LIFE (article) by Thomas Carey.

Penny Illustrated Paper. (P.I.P.)

2586–2587 17 Dec. 1910 to 24 Dec. 1910 THE MURDER AT

THE 'PORTHELM' (My name is Thomas Carlyle Smith . . .)

The People

23 Dec. 1923 to 6 Apr. 1924 THE FELLOWSHIP (A dry radiator coincided with a burst tyre . . .)

BK   *The Fellowship of the Frog*

Series 'Wonderful London'

13 Apr. 1924 1. THE GIRL IN THE NIGHT CLUB RAID (There are generally two sides to every . . .

20 Apr. 1924 2. THE EASTER MONDAY PRINCE (When the master of the household . . .)

27 Apr. 1924 3. THE GIRL WHO WON AT EPSOM (When Alicia Penton entered the . . .)

MG   *E.W.M.M.* (Br,) No. 34, May 1967. The Girl who won at Epsom.

4 May 1924 4. THE VAMPIRE OF WEMBLEY (The Gentle Tressa was remarkable . . .)

MG   *E.W.M.M.* (Br), No. 33, April 1967. The Wimbledon Vampire.

11 May 1924 5. THE MAN BEHIND THE OPERA (Miss Isobel Howard! . . .)

18 May 1924 6. THE PICTURE OF THE YEAR (You could count on the fingers of . . .)

25 May 1924 7. PRESENTED AT COURT (Daphne Wyse found Scarlatti's . . .)

1 June 1924 8. A DEAL ON THE DERBY (I feel rather guilty about . . .)

8 June 1924 9. WIMBLEDON AND A WOMAN ('For Miss Howard' . . .)

15 June 1924 10. AN ASCOT ADVENTURE (I always think Miss Howard . . .)

198

22 June 1924 11. AN OLYMPIC INTERLUDE
(Having performed to her own satisfaction)

29 June 1924 12. A HOUSEBOAT AT HENLEY
(Daphne propped up in the best . . .)

6 July 1924 13. A GOODWOOD GUEST (Most of
the Women at the dinner . . .)

13 July 1924 14. A DEAUVILLE GAMBLE (Do
you know Peter, said Daphne . . .)

20 July 1924 15. A HARROGATE ATTACHMENT
(The Doctor says it is gout . . .)

27 July 1924 16. A MATTER OF PREFERENCE
(Look here Wilmot said the Hon. Gervaise . . .)

6 Dec. 1925 to May 23 1926 THE GALLOWS
HAND (Harry the lancer came into Burton . . .)

BK   The Terrible People

14 Feb. 1932 A VERY DECENT MAN 'EDGAR
WALLACE' (article by Hannan Swaffer.)

Premier Magazine

The Worst Man in the World

1922

144   THE FIRST CRIME (When I left Dartmoor
        Prison . . .)

145   THE SNAKE WOMAN (I always think and speak
        of her . . .)

146   ON THE CORNISH EXPRESS (The average warder
        is . . .)

147   THE MASTER CRIMINAL (Is there a real master
        criminal . . .)

148   THE HOUSE OF DOOM (I should very much like
        to meet . . .)

149   THE LAST CRIME (The last time I came out of
        prison . . .)

Red Magazine (Amalgamated Press)

Gospel Truth Mortimer

126	1 July 1914 HIS START IN LIFE (when a millionaire receives a letter)
127	15 July 1914 THE SIX BLUE RINGS (Mr. Chell, that parsimonious millionaire . . .)
128	1 Aug. 1914 AS CHEAP AS WATER (There is one man in the world . . .)
129	15 Aug. 1914 THE AGENT OF KINGS (One evening when Gospel Truth Mortimer . . .)

Royal Magazine (C. Arthur Pearson)

Nov. 1914 TURNING OUT A 'TOMMY' (article)

Dec. 1914 UNDER FIRE (article)

Jan. 1915 NOBBY—THE INTERPRETER ('In this world', said Private Smith . . .)

BK   *Smithy and the Hun*. The Interpreter.

Feb. 1915 NOBBY—WHEN NOBBY WAS A WEATHER PROPHET ('If you were to ask me . . .)

BK   *Smithy and the Hun*. The Weather Prophet.

Mar. 1915 NOBBY—NOBBY TAKES TO LETTER WRITING ('Hows them war correspondents . . .)

BK   *Smithy and the Hun*. The Letter Writer.

Apr. 1915 NOBBY—NOBBY IN ROMANTIC VEIN ('Nobby Clark wrote a poem of hate once . . .)

BK   *Smithy and the Hun*. Nobby in Romantic Vein.

May 1915 NOBBY—JAM FOR THE ENEMY ('There's ten ways of finishing the war . . .)

June. 1915 NOBBY—ON BETTING COMMISSIONS ('There was a feller . . .)

BK   *Smithy and the Hun*. On Recruiting.

Feb. 1916 WRINKLES FOR RECRUITS (article) ('It may or not be true . . .)

Aug. 1916 WOMAN THE WARRIOR (article)

Dec. 1919 THERE IS NOTHING WRONG WITH US (article) (News is trouble . . .)

Feb. 1920 THE MAN WHO KILLED HIMSELF (Preston Somerville was standing . . .)

BK   *Forty Eight Short Stories*. The Man who Killed Himself.

BK   *The Little Green Man*. The Man who Killed Himself.

Mar. 1920 MOTHER O' MINE (They called Ian Cranford . . .)

BK   *Forty Eight Short Stories*. Mother o' Mine.

BK   *The Governor of Chi-Foo*. Mother o' Mine.

Feb. 1921 THE MAN WHO MARRIED HIS COOK (One afternoon in May . . .)

BK   *The Lady called Nita*. The Man who married his cook.

Aug. 1921 THE LIMP OF CLAN CHEN (The pace of his excellency Chi Li Chen . . .)

MG   *Thriller*, 316, 23 Feb. 1935. The Limp of Clan Chen.

Dec. 1921 THE TRUST IN PRINCES (Mr. Benjamin Thanet was a . . .)

MG   *Pearsons Magazine*, 2064, 15 Feb. 1930. For the King's Comfort.

MG   *Wild West Weekly*, No. 7, 23 Apr. 1938. The King who chased Butterflies.

Apr. 1922 JAKE'S BROTHER BILL (The effect of wine . . .)

BK   *Forty Eight Short Stories*. Jake's Brother Bill.

BK   *The Governor of Chi-Foo*. Jake's Brother Bill.

Aug. 1922 THE EAR OF THE SANCTUARY (When men in all sincerity . . .)

BK	*For Information Received*. The Ear of the Sanctuary.
	Sept. 1922 ONE WITH AUTHORITY. (Pamela Wilson once lectured . . .)
BK	*The Lady of Little Hell*. The Cross of the Thief.
	Mar. 1923 LURE OF STRANGE GODS. (Between Camden Town . . .)
BK	*For Information Received*. A Priestess of Osiris.
	July 1923 WHAT OF THE YOUNG MEN? (Once upon a time there lived a chef . . .) (article showing large photo of Edgar Wallace)
	Nov. 1928 EDGAR WALLACE THE MAN by R. G. Curtis.
	1929 HE WHO COULD RIDE (Colonel Desboro was an easy . . .)
BK	*Fighting Snub Reilly*. The Christmas Cup.
BK	*Forty Eight Short Stories*. The Christmas Cup.
MG	*E.W.M.M.* (Br.), 29, Dec. 1966. The Christmas Cup.
MG	*Windsor Magazine*, Vol. 63, Dec. 1925 to May 1926. The Christmas Cup.
BK	*The Undisclosed Client*. The Christmas Cup.
	1929 WHEN THE WORLD STOPPED. (Mr. Herbert Fallowill made his final . . .)

New Royal Magazine

No. 1.	Dec. 1930 MR. JIGGS MAKES GOOD. (Mr. Denny of Lansfield . . .)
BK	*The Last Adventure*. Mr. Jiggs makes Good.

The Saint Detective Magazine (British Edition)

	Nov. 1954 THE MAGIC OF FEAR (All this happened in the interim . . .)
BK	*Sanders*. The Magic of Fear.

Apr. 1955 DISHONOUR AMONG THIEVES (When I was a steward on . . .)

Sep. 1955 THE POETICAL POLICEMAN (The day Mr. Reeder arrived . . ..)

BK   *The Mind of Mr. J. G. Reeder.* The Poetical Policeman.

MG   *Thriller*, 304, 1st Dec. 1934. The Poet Policeman.

MG   *Grand Magazine*, Vol. 46, Sept. 1924 to Feb. 1925. The Strange Case of the Night Watchman.

BK   *Fifty Famous Detectives of Fiction.* The Poetical Policeman.

Jan. 1956 THE TREASURE OF MR. REEDER (There is a tradition in criminal)

BK   *The Mind of Mr. J. G. Reeder.* The Treasure Hunt.

MG   *Thriller*, 287, 4th Aug. 1934. The Treasure Hunt.

MG   *Grand Magazine*, Vol. 46, Sept. 1924 to Feb. 1925. The Treasure Hunt.

Aug. 1956 THE DISAPPEARING INVESTORS (There are seven million people)

BK   *The Mind of Mr. J. G. Reeder.* The Investors.

MG   *Thriller*, 294, 22nd Sept. 1934. The Investors.

MG   *E.W.M.M.* (Br), No. 25, Aug. 1966. They walked away.

MG   *Grand Magazine*, Vol. 47, Mar. to Aug. 1925. The Investors.

Feb. 1959 THE MAN WHO SANG IN CHURCH (To Leon Gonsalez went most of the)

BK   *Again the Three Just Men.* The Man who Sang in Church.

MG   20 *Story Magazine*, Sept. 1927. The Man who Sang in Church.

Apr. 1959 THE HAPPY TRAVELLERS (Of the three men who had . . .)

BK   *Again the Three Just Men*. The Happy Travellers.

June 1959 THE DEADLY MR. LYON (There is water in the Great . . .)

BK   *Sergeant Sir Peter*. Buried Treasure.

MG   *Strand Magazine*, May 1930. Buried Treasure.

Oct. THE FORTUNE OF FORGERY (The Man who reclined . . .)

BK   *Again the Ringer*. The Fortune of Forgery.

Nov. 1960 THE ENGLISHMAN KONNER (The Three Just Men sat longer . . .)

BK   *Again the Three Just Men*. The Englishman Konner.

MG   20 *Story Magazine*, Jan. 1928. The Englishman Konner.

Jul. 1962 THE SLANE MYSTERY (The Killing of Bernard Slane . . .)

BK   *Again the Three Just Men*. The Slane Mystery.

Sep. 1962 THE BLACK GRIPPE (Dr. Hereford Bevan was looking . . .)

MG   *Strand Magazine*, Mar. 1920. The Black Grippe.

Jan. 1963 CHRISTMAS BONDAGE (who knows where I may sleep tonight . . .)

BK   *The Governor of Chi-Foo*. In Thrall.

BK   *Forty Eight Short Stories*. In Thrall.

MG   *Grand Magazine*

Mar. 1963 THE MAN WHO HATED AMELIA JONES (There was a letter that came . . .)

BK   *The Law of the Four Just Men*. The man who hated Amelia Jones.

MG   *Strand Magazine*, Sept. 1921. The man who hated Amelia Jones.

Oct. 1963 THE MAN WITH THE CANINE TEETH
(Murder my dear Manfred . . .)

BK   *The Law of the Four Just Men*. The Man with the Canine Teeth.

MG   *Strand Magazine*, June. 1921. The Man with the Canine Teeth.

May 1964 THE LITTLE BARONESS (when you're twentyone . . .)

BK   *The Steward*. The Little Baroness.

MG   *Grand Magazine*, Vol. 49, Mar to Aug. 1926. The Little Baroness.

Apr. 1965 THE MAN WHO DIED TWICE (The interval between acts II and III)

BK   *The Law of the Four Just Men*. The Man who died Twice.

MG   *Strand Magazine*, Aug. 1921. The Man who died Twice.

Sporting Pink Holiday Annual

1910 WITH A GUIDE IN FLUSHING (Poem)

1911 HOW I WON THE DERBY (Poem)

Story Teller (Cassells)

July 1907 SMITHY'S BEST GIRL (Smithy sat on the Canteen Table . . .)

BK   *Nobby*. Nobby's Best Girl.

March 1908 THE MONKEY AND THE BOX (When Christopher Angle went to school he . . .)

June 1910 THE SILVER CHARM (Angel, Esquire, has a little office . . .)

MG   *Harmsworth's All Story Magazine*, Aug. 1927. The Silver Charm.

BK   *The Woman from the East*. The Silver Charm.

Apr. 1913 THE SUFFRAGISTS HUSBAND (Claude Galloway sat at breakfast . . .)

July 1913 UNCLE FARAWAY (It was thirty years since the Man . . .)

BK *The Woman from the East.* Uncle Faraway.

Strand Magazine (Newnes)

July to Dec. 1914 THE DESPATCH RIDER (Lady Galigay was always . . .)

Jan. to June. 1916 CODE NO. 2 (The Secret Service never . . .)

BK *Forty Eight Short Stories.* Code No. 2.
BK *The Little Green Man.* Code No. 2.
MG *E.W.M.M.* (Br), No. 22, May 1966. Code No. 2.

Vol. 58 Aug. 1919 MR. MILLER AND THE KAISER (Against the Day when . . .)
Sept. 1919 IF—?
The Story of the 'Joy Bell' comedy scene by Albert de Courville & Edgar Wallace which starred George Robey & Shirley Kellogg.

Mar. 1920 THE BLACK GRIPPE (Dr. Hereford Bevan was looking . . .)

MG *Saint Mag.* (Br), Sept. 1962. The Black Grippe.

May 1920 THE MAN WHO CAME BACK
The Story of the much discussed sketch of the new de Courville play, Whirligig.

May 1921 THE MAN WHO LIVED AT CLAPHAM
BK *The Law of the Four Just Men.* The Man who lived at Clapham.

June 1921 THE MAN WITH THE CANINE TEETH
BK *The Law of the Four Just Men.* The Man with the Canine Teeth.

MG	*Saint Mag.* (Br.), Oct. 1963. The Man with the Canine Teeth.

July 1921 THE MAN WHO HATED EARTH WORMS

BK	*The Law of the Four Just Men.* The Man who hated Earth Worms.

Aug. 1921 THE MAN WHO DIED TWICE

BK	*The Law of the Four Just Men.* The Man who died Twice.
MG	*Saint Mag.* (Br.), Apr. 1965. The Man who died Twice.

Sept. 1921 THE MAN WHO HATED AMELIA JONES

MG	*Saint Magazine* (Br.), Mar. 1963. The Man who hated Amelia Jones.

Oct. 1921 THE MAN WHO WAS HAPPY

BK	*The Law of the Four Just Men.* The Man who was Happy.

Dec. 1921 THE DEAR LIAR (Sylvia Crest walked back to her . . .)

BK	*Forty Eight Short Stories.* The Dear Liar.
BK	*Circumstantial Evidence.* The Dear Liar.

Jan. 1922 FIGHTING SNUB REILLY (Few minutes before Snub Reilly . . .)

BK	*Fighting Snub Reilly.* Fighting Snub Reilly.
BK	*Forty Eight Short Stories.* Fighting Snub Reilly.

Aug. 1922 CIRCUMSTANTIAL EVIDENCE (Colonel Chartres Dane lingered . . .)

BK	*Circumstantial Evidence.* Circumstantial Evidence.
BK	*Forty Eight Short Stories.* Circumstantial Evidence.
MG	E.W.M.M. (Br.), No. 9, Apr. 1965. Circumstantial Evidence.
BK	*Black Cap.* Circumstantial Evidence.

Aug. 1924 THE MIND OF A RACE-HORSE (article)

June. 1929 THE BUSINESS SIDE OF RACING (article)

Dec. 1929 THE FOUR MISSING MERCHANTS (Peter Dunn walked into his . . .)
BK   *Sergeant Sir Peter*. The Four Missing Merchants.

Jan. 1930 THE DESK BREAKER
BK   *Sergeant Sir Peter*. The Desk Breaker.

Feb. 1930 THE INHERITOR
BK   *Sergeant Sir Peter*. The Inheritor.

Mar. 1930 DR. FIFER'S PATIENT
BK   *Sergeant Sir Peter*. Dr. Fifer's Patient.

Apr. 1930 THE BURGLAR ALARM
BK   *Sergeant Sir Peter*. The Burglar Alarm.

May 1930 BURIED TREASURE
BK   *Sergeant Sir Peter*. Buried Treasure.
MG   *Saint Mag.* (Br.), July 1959. The Deadly Mr. Lyon.

June. 1930 THE PRINCIPLES OF JO LOLESS
BK   *Sergeant Sir Peter*. The Principles of Jo Loless.

1932 THE WINNING TICKET (From her point of observation . . .)
BK   *The Last Adventure*. The Winning Ticket.

Sunday Graphic and Sunday News articles

854   16 Aug. 1931 THE STRANGE CASE OF THE POISONED PARTRIDGE

855   23 Aug. 1931. THE MAN BEHIND THE GUN

856   30 Aug. 1931 THIS IS HEAVEN

857   6 Sept. 1931 UNKNOWN MURDERERS

858	13 Sept. 1931 IS ANYONE WORTH £6,000 A WEEK
859	20 Sept. 1931 BEWARE OF THE WRONG KIND OF ECONOMY
860	27 Sept. 1931 IN THE SHADOW OF THE MIGHTY COLOSSEUM AT ROME
861	4 Oct. 1931 IF NOBODY PAID UP
862	11 Oct. 1931 MY WAY WITH GANGSTERS
863	18 Oct. 1931 DEBUNKING THE CRIMINAL
864	25 Oct. 1931 THE PLAYWRIGHTS SECRET
865	1 Nov. 1931 THE GAMBLER
866	8 Nov. 1931 A JOB FOR THE POLICE
867	15 Nov. 1931 FILMS OF THE FUTURE
868	22 Nov. 1931 THE JUDGE'S MILE
869	29 Nov. 1931 MURDERER'S I WOULD NOT HANG
871	13 Dec 1931 BABIES ARE IN THE FRONT LINE
872	20 Dec. 1931. YOU CAN'T KILL CRIME BY PETTING THUGS
873	27 Dec 1931 RAMP ON THE RACKET
874	3 Jan. 1932 BLUEBEARD'S WOMEN
880	14 Feb. 1932 Last article Written by Edgar Wallace. No title but dealt with Gangsters.

*Sunday Journal** (London Publishing Company)

> *Serial Commenced*
> 2 Mar. 1909 'O.C.'
> (A Soldiers Love Story)

*Copies of this publication are unobtainable from the files of the British Museum, and as the publishers are no longer in existence no further information can be given.

H

Sunday News
Sir Arthur Conan Doyle has suggested that trained Clair-voyants whom he calls 'Aerial Bloodhounds' should be engaged to aid Scotland Yard in the detection of crime: Edgar Wallace replies:

4524	25 Aug. 1929 EDGAR WALLACE AND 'AERIAL BLOODHOUNDS'
4525	1 Sept. 1929 Sir Arthur Conan Doyle Replies.
4526	8 Sept. 1929 'MEDIUMS' CANNOT SOLVE CRIME MYSTERIES by Edgar Wallace
4527	15 Sept. 1929 Sir Arthur Conan Doyle Replies.

With No. 4602, 22 Feb. 1931, Edgar Wallace appointed editor.

4602	22 Feb. 1931 WELCOMING NEW EDITOR (article)
4603	1 Mar. 1931 SIR JOHN SIMON SPEAKS OUT TO EDGAR WALLACE (article)
4604	8 Mar. 1931 LORD BEAVERBROOK SPEAKS THE TRUTH (article)
4605	15 Mar. 1931 TO HANG OR NOT TO HANG (article)
4606	22 Mar. 1931 THE NEW CRIME (article) THE MAN IN THE DITCH (As I came through Windthorn . . .) (Missing word competition)
4607	29 Mar. 1931 THE TRUTH ABOUT LLOYD GEORGE (article)
4608	5 Apr. 1931 AL CAPONE (article) THE CHILDREN'S HOUR (Hurt and silent . . .) (Missing word competition)
4609	12 Apr. 1931 THE KING (article)
4610	19 Apr. 1931 THE DUSSELDORF HOOK (article)

4611	26 Apr. 1931 THE PRINCE (article)
4612	3 May 1931 MONEY FOR FILMS (article)
4613	10 May 1931 I MEET A GHOST (article)
4614	17 May 1931 BLACKMAIL (article)
4615	24 May 1931 MY FIRST FIVE FOR THE DERBY (article)
4616	31 May 1931 WHERE IS MY BEAUTIFUL SCREEN GIRL (article)
4617	7 June 1931 WILL MR. CLYNES PROSECUTE LLOYDS BANK ? (article)
4618	14 June 1931 WHO ARE THE BISHOPS (article)
4619	21 June 1931 IF GERMANY FAILS (article)
4620	28 June 1931 BUT OUR OWN WAR BURDENS (article)
4621	5 July 1931 THE BLUE-PRINTS OF CIVILISATION (article)
4622	12 July 1931 ROT ABOUT POLICE SCANDALS (article) **The Chair** First of a series of crime article followed by other writers
4623	19 July 1931 IS IT TO BE WAR (article)
4624	26 July 1931 IF I WERE A CROOK (article)
4625	2 Aug. 1931 RONALD LOTRUE—THE TRUTH! (article)
4626	9 Aug. 1931 THE IMMORAL LONDON RUBBISH (article) *(now incorporated into Sunday Graphic)*

Thomsons Weekly News (D. C. Thomson Ltd.)

3271–3288	26 Jan. 1918 to 25 May 1918 MY ADVENTURES AS A GERMAN SPY—IN BRITAIN By Hermann Gallwitz, agent for Captain Karl von Rinlellen the famous Banker Spy, written and edited by Edgar Wallace.

3289–3297	1 June 1918 to 27 July 1918 MAJOR HAYNES OF THE SECRET SERVICE
	Real life stories from the notes of Captain Dane, his Chief of Staff, by Edgar Wallace.
3308	12 Oct. 1918 WHAT HAPPENED AT HUN HEAD-QUARTERS (article)
3312	9 Nov. 1918 IF GERMANY HAD WON THE WAR (article)
3315	30 Nov. 1918 'COMRADE' HINDENBURG AND THE SOVIET (story)
3316	7 Dec. 1911 'COMRADE' HINDENBURG VISITS THE KAISER (story)
3319	28 Dec. 1918 THE KAISER IN THE WITNESS-BOX (story)
3326	15 Feb. 1919 THE GREAT WIFE STRIKE (article)
3334	12 Apr. 1919 AMAZING TRICKS I HAVE SEEN PERFORMED (article)

Thriller (Amalgamated Press)

1	9 Feb. 1929 RED ACES
BK	*Red Aces*. Red Aces.
3	23 Feb. 1929 KENNEDY THE CON MAN
BK	*Red Aces*. Kennedy the Con Man.
7	23 Mar. 1929 THE CROOK IN CRIMSON
51	25 Jan. 1930 THE FATAL CULT
53	8 Feb. 1930 GUV'NORS ORDERS
105	7 Feb. 1931 THE MAN FROM SING-SING
BK	*The Guv'nor and Other Stories*. The Man who passed.
106	14 Feb. 1931 THE PRISONER OF SEVENWAYS
BK	*The Guvnor and Other Stories*. The Treasure House.
BK	*Mr. J. G. Reeder Returns*. The Treasure House.
156	30 Jan. 1932 THE SHADOW MAN

BK	*Mr. J. G. Reeder Returns*. The Shadow Man.
BK	*The Guv'nor and Other Stories*. The Shadow Man.
158	13 Feb. 1932 THE DEATH WATCH
BK	*Sergeant Sir Peter*. The Death Watch.
286	28 July 1934 THE STRETELLI CASE
BK	*Forty Eight Short Stories*. The Stretelli Case.
BK	*The Little Green Man*. The Stretelli Case.
BK (Digit)	*The Terror*. The Stretelli Case.
287	4 Aug. 1934 THE TREASURE HUNT
BK	*The Mind of Mr. J. G. Reeder*. The Treasure Hunt.
MG	*Saint Magazine* (Br.), Jan. 1956. The Treasure of Mr. Reeder.
MG	*Grand Magazine*, Vol. 46, Sept. 1924 to Feb. 1925. The Treasure Hunt.
288	11 Aug. 1934 THE PRISON BREAKERS
BK	*Forty Eight Short Stories*. The Prison Breakers.
BK	*The Prison Breakers*. The Prison Breakers.
MG	*E.W.M.M.* (Br.), No. 30, Jan. 1967. The Prison Breakers.
289	18 Aug. 1934 SHEER MELODRAMA
BK	*The Mind of Mr. J. G. Reeder*. Sheer Melodrama.
MG	*E.W.M.M.* (Br.), No. 27, Oct. 1966. Sheer Melodrama.
MG	*Grand Magazine*, Vol. 47, Mar. to Aug. 1925. The Man from the East.
290	25 Aug. 1934 THE MAN WHO NEVER LOST
BK	*Forty Eight Short Stories*. The Man Who Never Lost.
BK	*The Little Green Man*. The Man Who Never Lost.
MG	*E.W.M.M.* (Br.), No. 11, June 1965. The Man Who Never Lost.

J

MG   *Town Topics*, 383/4, 27 Dec. 1919 to 3 Jan. 1920, The Man Who Never Lost.

291   1 Sept. 1934 THE MEDIEVAL MIND (There can be no question . . .)
BK   *Forty Eight Short Stories*. The Medieval Mind.
BK   *Circumstantial Evidence*. The Medieval Mind.

292   8 Sept. 1934 THE GREEN MAMBA
BK   *The Mind of Mr. J. G. Reeder*. The Green Mamba.
MG   *Grand Magazine*, Vol. 47, Mar. to Aug. 1925. Ths Dangerous Reptile.

293   15 Sept. 1934 INDIAN MAGIC
BK   *Forty Eight Short Stories*. Indian Magic.
BK   *Circumstantial Evidence*. Indian Magic.

294   22 Sept. 1934 THE INVESTORS
BK   *The Mind of Mr. J. G. Reeder*. The Investors.
MG   *E.W.M.M.* (Br), No. 25, Aug. 1966. They Walked Away.
MG   *Saint Magazine* (Br), Aug. 1956. The Disappearing Investors.
MG   *Grand Magazine*, Vol. 47, Mar to Aug. 1925. The Investors.

304   1 Dec. 1934 THE POET POLICEMAN
BK   *The Mind of Mr. J. G. Reeder*. The Poetical Policeman.
BK   *Fifty Famous Detectives of Fiction*. The Poetical Policeman.
MG   *Saint Magazine* (Br), Sept. 1955. The Poetical Policeman.
MG   *Grand Magazine*, Vol. 46, Sept. 1924 to Feb. 1925. The Strange Case of the Night Watchman.

307   22 Dec. 1935 THE REMARKABLE MR. REEDER
BK   *The Mind of Mr. J. G. Reeder*. The Troupe.

MG	*E.W.M.M.* (Br), No. 16 Nov. 1965. The Remarkable Mr. Reeder.
MG	*Grand Magazine*, Vol. 46. Sept. 1924 to Feb. 1925. A Place on the River.
312	26 Jan. 1935 WHITE STOCKING
BK	*Forty Eight Short Stories*. White Stocking.
BK	*The Cat Burglar*. White Stocking.
MG	*Grand Magazine*, Vol. 41, Mar. to Aug. 1922. White Stocking.
N	*Evening Standard*, 6 June 1934. White Stocking.
316	23 Feb. 1935 THE LIMP OF CLAN CHEN
MG	*Royal Magazine*, Aug. 1921. The Limp of Clan Chen.
317	2 Mar. 1935 THE POISONERS
319	16 Mar. 1935 THE MAN WHO LOVED MUSIC
BK	*The Law of the Four Just Men*. The Man Who Loved Music.
MG	*Novel Magazine*, Sept. 1921. The Man who loved music.
321	30 Mar. 1935 THE MAN WHO WOULD NOT SPEAK
BK	*The Law of the Four Just Men*. The Man Who Would Not Speak.
MG	*Novel Magazine*, Aug. 1921. The Man Who Would Not Speak.
325	27 Feb. 1935 THE MAN WHO WAS PLUCKED
BK	*The Law of the Four Just Men*. The Man Who Was Plucked.
335	6 July 1935 THE MAN WHO WAS AQUITTED
BK	*The Law of the Four Just Men*. The Man Who Was Aquitted.
337	20 July 1935 THE NERVE OF TONY NEWTON
BK	*The Brigand*. A Matter of Nerve.

| 344 | 7 Sept. 1935 TONY NEWTON BOOKMAKER |
| BK | *The Brigand*. Anthony the Bookmaker. |

| 345 | 14 Sept. 1935 THE GOLDEN BAIT |

357	7 Dec. 1935 VOTE FOR TONY NEWTON
BK	*The Brigand*. The Bursted Election.
MG	*Novel Magazine*, Feb. 1923. The Bursted Election.

358	14 Dec. 1935 THE JOKE OF A LIFETIME
BK	*The Brigand*. The Joker.
MG	*Novel Magazine*, March 1923. The Joker.

| 359 | 21 Dec. 1935 THE DUCHESS IN DISTRESS |

| 415 | 16 Jan. 1937 THE TORN CHEQUE |

Topical Times (D. C. Thomson)

487	16 Mar. 1939 THE POISONED CUP (They called Chief Inspector Oliver Rater . . .)
BK	*The Orator*. The Orator.
MG	*Pall Mall Magazine*, 4, Aug. 1927. The Orator.

488	23 Mar. 1929 THE MIND READERS (There is no police force in the world . . .)
BK	*The Orator*. The Mind Readers.
MG	*Pall Mall Magazine*, 6, Oct. 1927. The Mind Readers.
N	*Evening Standard*, 5 Aug. 1935. The Mind Readers.
BK	*Fifty Famous Detectives of Fiction*. The Mind Readers.

489	30 Mar. 1929 THE OLD LADY WHO CHANGED HER MIND (Mr. Rater never took a job . . .)
BK	*The Orator*. The Old Lady who changed her mind.
MG	*Pall Mall Magazine*, 5, Sept. 1927. The Old Lady who changed her mind.

MG	*Pall Mall Magazine*, 13, May 1928. The Guy from Memphis.
MG	*E.W.M.M.* (Br.), No. 15, Sept. 1966. The Guy from Memphis.
497	25 May 1929 THE DETECTIVE WHO TALKED (Let me say at first I was never . . .)
BK	*The Orator*. The Detective who talked.
MG	*Pall Mall Magazine*, 15, July 1928. The Detective who Talked.
498	1 June 1929 THE FALL OF MR. RATER (The Orator was a man who had very . . .)
BK	*The Orator*. The Fall of Mr. Rater.
MG	*Pall Mall Magazine*, 14, June 1928. The Orators Downfall.

The Scallywags all slightly revised from the Mixer stories

511	31 Aug. 1929 THE OUTWITTING OF PONY NELSON (Pony Nelson had Clicked . . .)
BK	*The Mixer*. The Outwitting of Pony Nelson.
512	7 Sept. 1929 THE GREAT GENEVA SWEEPSTAKE (Graeside is a very . . .)
BK	*The Mixer*. The Great Geneva Sweepstake.
513	14 Sept. 1929 A SPECULATION IN SHARES (In one of the most fashionable . . .)
BK	*The Mixer*. A Speculation in shares.
514	21 Sept. 1929 THE BANK THAT DID NOT FAIL (A young man walked endlessly . . .)
BK	*The Mixer*. The Bank that did not fail.
515	28 Sept. 1929 MR. LIMMERBURG'S WATERLOO (Good said Sam putting . . .)
BK	*The Mixer*. Mr. Limmerburg's Waterloo.
516	5 Oct. 1929 HOW A FAMOUS MASTER CRIMINAL WAS TRAPPED
BK	*The Mixer*. How a Famous Criminal was Trapped.

517 12 Oct. 1929 A CLOSE CALL—AND ITS SEQUEL (Miss Millicent K. Yonker was a . . .)

BK *The Mixer*. A Close Call—and its Sequel.

518 19 Oct. 1929 MR. SPARKES, THE DETECTIVE (Do you remember Millicent K. Yonker . . .)

BK *The Mixer*. Mr. Sparkes, the Detective.

519 26 Oct. 1929 THE SUBMARINE-CHASER COUP (There's one thing that worries)

BK *The Mixer*. The Submarine-Chaser Coup.

520 2 Nov. 1929 A STRANGE FILM ADVENTURE Bilbao on a hot day . . .)

BK *The Mixer*. A Strange Film Adventure.

The Return of the Scallywags

530 11 Jan. 1930 THE GIRL FROM GIBRALTAR (Baltimore Jones had cleaned)

BK *The Mixer*. The Girl from Gibraltar.

531 18 Jan. 1930 THE SILK STOCKINGS (A Few days after cousin Bessie . . .)

BK *The Mixer*. The Silk Stockings.

532 25 Jan. 1930 THE SEVENTY-FOURTH DIAMOND (The Stolid looking Inspector)

BK *The Mixer*. The Seventy-Fourth Diamond.

533 1 Feb. 1930 ON THE MOVIES (Sam said Saul curiously . . .)

BK *The Mixer*.

534 8 Feb. 1930 THE CROWN JEWELS (Sandy had said bitterly . . .)

BK *The Mixer*. The Crown Jewels.

535 15 Feb. 1930 THE SPANISH PRISONER (as already indicated . . .)

BK *The Mixer*. The Spanish Prisoner.

536 22 Feb. 1930 THE CASE OF DOLLY DE MULLE (The organisation of the . . .)

BK	*The Mixer*. The Case of Dolly de Mulle.
537	1 Mar. 1930 THE PROFESSOR (The Anglo-American Sugar . . .)
BK	*The Mixer*. The Professor.

Town Topics

102	8 Aug. 1914 LONDON AT WAR! (article) TO THE SERVICE
MG	*Town Topics*, 235, 24 Feb. 1917 To the Service.
106	5 Sept. 1914 THE COLONIAL TROOPS (poem 28 lines)
107	12 Sept. 1914 GUNS AT LE CATEAU (poem)
108	19 Sept. 1914 SMITHY (short story)
109	26 Sept. 1914 SOLDIER SONGS 1 (poem) SMITH SURVEYS THE LAND (short story ½ page)
BK	*Smithy and the Hun*. Smithy Surveys the Land.
110	3 Oct. 1914 THE MIDNIGHT LIST (poem)
111	10 Oct. 1914 SOLDIER SONGS 2 (poem) SMITHY ON DESPATCH WRITING (short story)
112	17 Oct. 1914 SOLDIER SONGS 3 (poem) SMITHY AND THE STRATEGIST (story)
113	25 Oct. 1914 SOLDIER SONGS 4 (poem) SMITHY AND THE MISSING ZEP'LINK (story)
BK	*Smithy and the Hun*. Smithy and the Missing Zep'link.
114	31 Oct. 1914 SOLDIER SONGS 5 (poem)
115	7 Nov. 1914 SMITHY IN THE STRICTEST CONFIDENCE (story)
116	14 Nov. 1914 SOLDIER SONGS 6 (poem)
117	21 Nov. 1914 SOLDIER SONGS 7 (poem) VON KLUCK'S NEPHEW GINGER (Smithy story)
BK	*Smithy and the Hun*. Von Luck's Nephew.

Town Topics

394   14 Mar 1920 RELATIONS (short story)

399   18 Apr. 1920 'K' (article)

400   25 Apr. 1920 'THE FOUR JUST MEN' AND
           IRELAND (article criticism and suggestions that
           his book was Political)

Note

1) There were many other poems published which Edgar
Wallace may have written but only those that had his
name or initials EW are listed.

2) Smithy stories varied between one column and a whole
page.

20 Story Magazine (Odhams Ltd.)

	Oct. 1922 BILL JONES AND MRS. WILLIAM JONES (Her eyes were sleepy eyes . . .)
BK	*Mrs. William Jones and Bill.* Mrs. William Jones and Bill.

	Nov. 1922 THE FEARFUL WORD (Look after the chickens . . .)
BK	*Bones of the River.* The Fearful Word.

	Dec. 1922 A LOVER OF DOGS (The mail boat had come into sight . . .)
BK	*Bones of the River.* A Lover of Dogs.

	Jan. 1923 A NICE GEL (Because Terence Doughty . . .)
BK	*Bones of the River.* A Nice Gel.

	Feb. 1923 THE BLACK EGG (Once upon a time in the Isisi Land . . .)
BK	*Bones of the River.* The Black Egg.

	Mar. 1923 THE MEDICAL OFFICER of HEALTH (For the use of Mr. Augustus Tibbetts . . .)
BK	*Bones of the River.* The Medical Officer of Health.

228

Apr. 1923 THE BRASS BEDSTEAD (There is no tribe in the river . . .)

BK   *Bones of the River*. The Brass Bedstead.

May 1923 THE CAMERA MAN (For a thousand years . . .)

BK   *Bones of the River*. The Camera Man.

June 1923 THE ALL AFRICANS (The mind of Mr. Commissioner Sanders . . .)

BK   *Bones of the River*. The All Africans.

July 1923 THE WAZOOS (When Bones brushed his hair . . .)

BK   *Bones of the River*. The Wazoos.

Aug. 1923 THE HEALER (Men lie with a certain transparent . . .)

BK   *Bones of the River*. The Healer.

Sept. 1923 THE WOMAN WHO SPOKE TO BIRDS (There was a man named . . .)

BK   *Bones of the River*. The Woman who Spoke to Birds.

Oct. 1923 THE LAKE OF THE DEVIL (M'Suru on Arkasava Chief . . .)

BK   *Bones of the River*. The Lake of the Devil.

Oct. 1924 SOLO AND THE LADY (I'm naturally fond of . . .)

BK   *The Steward*. Solo and the Lady.

The Further Adventures of the Three Just Men

Sept. 1927 THE MAN WHO SANG IN CHURCH (To Leon Gonsalez went most of the . . .)

BK   *Again the Three Just Men*. The Man who sang in Church.

MG   *Saint Magazine* (Br), Feb. 1959. The Man who sang in Church.

Oct. 1927 THE LADY FROM BRAZIL (The journey had begun in a . . .)

BK   *Again the Three Just Men*. The Lady from Brazil.

Nov. 1927 THE TYPIST WHO SAW THINGS (About every six months . . .)

BK   *Again the Three Just Men*. The Typist who saw things.

Dec. 1927 THE MYSTERY OF MR. DRAKE (All events go in threes . . .)

BK   *Again the Three Just Men*. The Mystery of Mr. Drake.

Jan. 1928 THE ENGLISHMAN KONNER (The Three Just Men sat longer . . .)

BK   *Again the Three Just Men*. The Englishman Konner.

MG   *Saint Magazine* (Br), Nov. 1960. The Englishman Konner.

Sept. 1929 THE DEATH ROOM (Do you believe in spiritualism . . .)

Oct. 1929 HER FATHER'S DAUGHTER (In the old days the Howarths . . .)

MG   *Nashes Illustrated Weekly*, No. 19, 17 Jan. 1920. A Girl among Thieves.

BK   *Lady Called Nita*. Her Father's Daughter.

Jan. 1930 THE PERFECT CRIMINAL (Mr. Felix O'Hara Golbeater . . .)

BK   *Forty Eight Short Stories*. The Compleat Criminal.

BK   *The Prison Breakers*. The Compleat Criminal.

BK   *The Thief in the Night* (Digit). The Compleat Criminal.

Jan. 1931 BULFOX ASLEEP (People Say that Bulfox was a fool . . .)

BK	*Forty Eight Short Stories*. Bulfox Asleep.
BK	*The Prison Breakers*. Bulfox Asleep.
MG	*Pearsons Weekly*, 1980, 7 July 1928. A Question of Honour.
MG	*Novel Magazine*, April 1913. A Question of Honour.

Union Jack 2nd Series (Amalgamated Press)

	1204 to 1219 13 Nov. 1926 to 28 Feb. 1927 THE THREE JUST MEN
BK	*The Three Just Men*

Weekly Tale Teller

2	15 May 1909 THE BANDAGED HAND (The Livingstone came thrashing down . . .)
4	29 May 1909 THE JUNIOR REPORTER (If the junior reporter approached the . . .)
21	25 Sept. 1909 THE WOOD OF DEVILS (Four days of M'Sakidanga . . .)
BK	*Sanders of the River*. The Wood of Devils.
23	9 Oct. 1909 THE LINCHELA REBELLION (As a variation of the tag . . .)
29	20 Nov. 1909 THE SPECIAL COMMISSIONER (The Hon. George Tackle had the . . .)
BK	*Sanders of the River*. The Special Commissioner.
36	8 Jan. 1910 THE DESTROYER (Over by Voisney and Heliograph . . .)
38	22 Jan. 1910 THE EXPLOITER (Sanders had graduated to West Central . . .)
BK	*Sanders of the River*. The Education of the King.
MG	*Novel Magazine*, Feb. 1912. The Education of the King.

43	26 Feb. 1910 THE EDUCATION OF KING PETER (In the land which curves along . . .)
BK	*Sanders of the River*. The Education of the King.
MG	Novel Magazine, Feb. 1912. The Education of the King.
46	19 Mar. 1910 BOSAMBO OF MONROVIA (For many years the Ochori people . . .)
BK	*Sanders of the River*. Bosambo of Monrovia.
51	23 April 1910. KEEPERS OF THE STONE (There is a people who live at Ochori . . .)
BK	*Sanders of the River*. Keepers of the Stone.
55	21 May 1910. HALLEY'S COMET, THE COWBOY, AND LORD DORRINGTON (Lord Dorrington was a middle aged . . .)
63	16 July 1910 DOGS OF WAR (Chiefest of the restrictions . . .)
BK	*Sanders of the River*. Dogs of War.
66	6 Aug. 1910 THE DANCING STONES (If any man believes . . .)
BK	*Sanders of the River*. The Dancing Stones.
76	15 Oct. 1910 THE STRANGER OF THE NIGHT (The little instrument on the table . . .)
BK	*The Woman from the East*. The Man of the Night.
81	19 Dec. 1910 THE GREEK POROPULOS (At Carolina in the Transvaal . . .)
BK	*Governor of Chi-Foo*. The Greek Poropulos.
BK	*Forty Eight Short Stories*. The Greek Poropulos.
MG	*E.W.M.M.* (Br.), No. 23, June 1966. The Killer of Lioski:
BK	The Thief in the Night (Digit): The Greek Poropulos.

Mr. Commissioner Sanders

160   25 May 1912 BRETHREN OF THE ORDER (Native men loved Sanders . . .)

BK   *People of the River*. Brethren of the Order.

The Ruler of the River

173   24 Aug. 1912 NINE TERRIBLE MEN (There were nine terrible men . . .)

BK   *People of the River*. Nine Terrible Men.

174   31 Aug. 1912 IN THE VILLAGE OF IRONS (I have a photograph of Sanders . . .)

BK   *People of the River*. The Village of Irons.

175   9 Sept. 1912 SANDERS MISSIONARY (There is a moral story . . .)

BK   *People of the River*. The Missionary.

176   14 Sept. 1912 THE QUEEN OF N'GOMBI (There are certain native traits . . .)

BK   *People of the River*. The Queen of the N'Gombi.

177   21 Sept. 1912 THE RISING OF THE AKASAVA (A Native alone may plumb . . .)

BK   *People of the River*. The Rising of the Akasava.

178   28 Sept. 1912 MR. COMMISSIONER BOSAMBO (Stretched out on his bunk . . .)

BK   *People of the River*. The Rising of the Akasava.

179   5 Oct. 1912 A MAKER OF SPEARS (North of the Akasava Country . . .)

BK   *People of the River*. The Maker of Spears.

180   12 Oct. 1912 THE SICKNESS MONGO (Sanders taught his people . . .)

BK   *People of the River*. The Sickness Mongo.

181   19 Oct. 1912 THE TELLER OF TALES (Ariboo told Saunders that . . .)

BK   *People of the River*. The Praying Moor.

182   26 Oct. 1912. THE CRIME OF SANDERS (It is a fine thing to . . .)

BK	*People of the River*. The Crime of Sanders.
183	2 Nov. 1912 THE RULER OF THE RIVER (Once upon a time a man . . .)
BK	*People of the River*. The Man on the Spot.
184	9 Nov. 1912 SPRING OF THE YEAR (The life of one of his Britannic . . .)
BK	*People of the River*. Spring of the Year.
197	8 Feb. 1913 ARACHI THE BORROWER (Many years ago the Monrovian . . .)
BK	*Bosambo of the River*. Arachi the Borrower.
MG	*Chums*, 1927/8. Arachi the Borrower.
201	8 Mar. 1913 THE TAX RESISTERS (Sanders took nothing for granted . . .)
BK	*Bosambo of the River*. The Tax Resisters.
MG	*Chums*, 1927/8. The Tax Resisters.
206	12 Apr. 1913 THE RISE OF THE EMPEROR (Tobolaka, the King of the Isisi)
BK	*Bosambo of the River*. The Rise of the Emperor.
MG	*Chums*, 1927/8. The Rise of the Emperor.
207	19 Apr. 1913 THE FALL OF TOBOLAKA (My poor soul! Said the Houssa . . .)
BK	*Bosambo of the River*. The Fall of the Emperor.
MG	*Chums*, 1927/8. The Fall of the Emperor.
213	31 May 1913 THE KILLING OF OLANDI (Chief of Sanders spies . . .)
BK	*Bosambo of the River*. The Killing of Olandi.
MG	*Chums*, 1927/8. The Killing of Olandi.
226	30 Aug. 1913 THE PEDOMETER (Bosambo, the Chief of the Ochori . . .)
BK	*Bosambo of the River*. The Pedometer.
MG	*Chums*, 1927/8. The Pedometer.
238	22 Nov. 1913 KING OF THE OCHORI (Bosambo was a Monrovian . . .)

BK	*Bosambo of the River*. The Brother of Bosambo
MG	*Chums*, 1927/8. The Brother of Bosambo.
239	29 Nov. 1913 THE CHAIR OF THE N'GOMBI (The N'Gombi people prized . . .)
BK	*Bosambo of the River*. The Chair of the N'Gombi.
MG	*Chums*, 1927/8 The Chair of the N'Gombi.
240	6 Dec. 1913 THE KI-CHU (The Messenger from Sakola . . .)
BK	*Bosambo of the River*. The Ki-Chu.
MG	*Chums*, 1927/8. The Ki-Chu.
241	13 Dec. 1913 THE WONDERFUL LOVER (Out of the waste came a long . . .)
BK	*Bosambo of the River*. The Child of Sacrifice.
MG	*Chums*, 1927/8. The Child of Sacrifice.
242	20 Dec. 1913 THEY (In the Akarti Country they . . .)
BK	*Bosambo of the River*. They.
MG	*Chums*, 1927/8. They.
243	27 Dec. 1913 BOSAMBO'S DEVILS (There is a saying amongst the . . .)
BK	*Bosambo of the River*. The Ambassadors.
MG	*Chums*, 1927/8. The Ambassadors.
259	18 Apr. 1914 THE MAN WHO KILLED X (I once knew a lady named . . .)
260	25 Apr. 1914 THE VOICE IN THE NIGHT (Lies I do not mind . . .)
261	2 May 1914 ONE WILLIAM SMITH (My Mr. Coss—Heaven knows . . .)
262	9 May 1914 A TILT WITH MAY (Poor William Smith . . .)
263	16 May 1914 AN ADVENTURE ON THE COTE D'ACURE (There was a man called . . .)

BK	*Bones.* Henry Hamilton Bones.
294	19 Dec. 1914 THE GREEN CROCODILE (Cala Cala, as they say, seven . . .)
BK	*Bones.* The Green Crocodile.
295	26 Dec. 1914 A RIGHT OF WAY (The borders of territories may be fixed . . .)
BK	*Bones.* A Right of Way.
296	2 Jan. 1915 THE STRANGER WHO WALKED BY NIGHT (Since the day when Lieutenant . . .)
BK	*Bones.* The Stranger who walked by Night.
337	16 Oct. 1915 THE PRAYING GIRL (The Girl drove into the Bahnhof . . .)
BK	*The Lady of Little Hill.* The Praying Girl.
357	4 Mar. 1916 BONES, SANDERS AND ANOTHER (To Isongo, which stands . . .)
BK	*The Keepers of the King's Peace.* Bones, Sanders and another.
365	29 April 1916 THE GREATER BATTLE (Milton folded his serviette . . .)
last issue	
MG	*Town Topics,* 224, 9 Dec. 1916. The Greater Fight.

The Weekly Telegraph (John Leng).

3370–3382	20 Nov. 1926 to 12 Feb. 1927 THE FEATHERED SERPENT (Applause from the big audience . . .)
BK	*The Feathered Serpent*

Wild West Weekly.

No. 7	23 Apr. 1938 THE KING WHO CHASED BUTTERFLIES. (Mr. Benjamin Thanet was a . . .)
MG	*Pearsons Weekly,* 2064, 15 Feb. 1930. For the King's Comfort.
MG	*Royal Magazine,* Dec. 1921. A Trust in Princes.

Windsor Magazine (Ward Lock).

Vol. 32   June to Nov. 1910 HIS GAME (The Ninth
          Guards were at dinner . . .)
BK   *The Last Adventure*. His Game.

Vol. 33   Dec. 1910 to May 1911 THE ADVENTURES OF
          GEORGE (George Gregory Sanworth was re-
          garded . . .)
BK   *Mrs. William Jones and Bill*. The Adventures
          of George.

Vol. 34   June to Nov. 1911 CARFEW 11 (It was an idea;
          even Jenkins . . .)
BK   *The Admirable Carfew*. Carfew 11.

Vol. 35   Dec. 1911 to May 1912 CARFEW, WITHINGTON
          AND CO, INVENTORS (Carfew could never
          quite . . .)
BK   *The Admirable Carfew*. Carfew, Withington
          and Co, Inventors.

Vol. 36   June to Nov. 1912 THE AGREEABLE COMPANY
          (Carfew was a man who attracted money . . .)
BK   *The Admirable Carfew*. The Agreeable Com-
          pany.
          CARFEW IS ADVISED (Carfew was young and
          he was rich . . .)
BK   *The Admirable Carfew*. Carfew is Advised.

Vol. 37   Dec. 1912 to May 1913 A DEAL IN RIFFS
          (Carfew had a house in Bloomsbury . . .)
BK   *The Admirable Carfew*. A Deal in Riffs.
          CARFEW ENTERTAINS (Very few people know
          the truth . . .)
BK   *The Admirable Carfew*. Carfew Entertains.
          THE ECCENTRIC MR. GOBLEHEIM (Carfew
          was no plodder . . .)
BK   *The Admirable Carfew*. The Eccentric Mr.
          Gobleheim.

Vol. 38	June to Nov. 1913 PATRIOTS (You must remember about Carfew . . .)
BK	*The Admirable Carfew*. Patriots.
	TOBBINS LIMITED. (Mr. Carfew's broker called him up . . .)
BK	*The Admirable Carfew*. Tobbins Limited.
Vol. 39	Dec. 1913 to May 1914. CARFEW—IMPRESARIO (A thousand pounds is a lot . . .)
BK	*The Admirable Carfew*. Carfew—Impresario.
	WHY GELDEN MADE A MILLION (In the days when Carfew was . . .)
Bk	*The Admirable Carfew*. Why Gelden made a Million.
	CARFEW PRODUCES (There is an uninteresting part to . . .)
BK	*The Admirable Carfew*. Carfew Produces.
	CARFEW AND THE 'MARY Q'. (What kindness of heart was . . .)
BK	*The Admiral Carfew*. Carfew and the 'Mary Q'.
Vol. 40	June to Nov. 1914 A MATTER OF BUSINESS (Only Carfew knows whether he was . . .)
BK	*The Admirable Carfew*. A Matter of Business.
	ONE AND SEVENPENCE HA'PENNY (Carfew sat in his study . . .)
BK	*The Admirable Carfew*. One and Sevenpence Ha'penny.
	THE MEN OF THE ALLIED ARMIES AND THEIR GREAT TRADITION (Namur—Malplaquet—Waterloo—Ou Denarde . . .) (Long Article.)
Vol. 44	June to Nov. 1916 THE BRANDING OF BONES
BK	*Keepers of the King's Peace*. Bones Changes his Religion.
	BONES AND THE WIRELESS

	THE SLEUTH
BK	*Lieutenant Bones* The Sleuth.
Vol. 47	Dec. 1917 to May 1918 THE BREAKING POINT
BK	*Lieutenant Bones*. The Breaking Point.
	THE FETISH STICK
BK	*Lieutenant Bones*. The Fetish Stick.
	THE LEGENDEER
BK	*Lieutenant Bones*. The Legendeer.
	THE MADNESS OF VALENTINE
BK	*Lieutenant Bones*. The Madness of Valentine
	THE PACIFIST
BK	*Lieutenant Bones*. The Pacifist.
	THE SON OF SANDI
BK	*Lieutenant Bones*. The Son of Sandi.
Vol. 48	June to Nov. 1918 KING ANDREAS
BK	*Lieutenant Bones*. King Andreas.
	THE LITTLE PEOPLE
BK	*Lieutenant Bones*. The Little People.
	THE NORTHERN MEN
BK	*Lieutenant Bones*. The Northern Men.
Vol. 51	Dec. 1919 to May 1920 BONES AND BIG BUSINESS
BK	*Bones in London*. Bones and Big Business.
	BONES AND THE WHARFINGERS
BK	*Bones in London*. Bones and the Wharfingers.
	A CINEMA PICTURE
BK	*Bones in London*. A Cinema Picture.
	A DEAL IN JUTE
BK	*Bones in London*. A Deal in Jute.
	HIDDEN TREASURE
BK	*Bones in London*. Hidden Treasure.
	THE LIGHT-PLOVER CAR
BK	*Bones in London*. The Plover-Light Car.

中

Vol. 52	June to Nov. 1920 A COMPETENT JUDGE OF POETRY
BK	*Bones in London*. A Competent Judge of Poetry.
	A STUDENT OF MEN
BK	*Bones in London*. A student of men.
	BONES HITS BACK
BK	*Bones in London*. Bones Hits Back.
	DETECTIVE BONES
BK	*Bones in London*. Detective Bones.
	THE BRANCH LINE
BK	*Bones in London*. The Branch Line.
	THE LAMP THAT NEVER WENT OUT
BK	*Bones in London*. The Lamp that never went out.
Vol. 53	Dec. 1920 to May 1921 THE PROPHETS OF THE OLD KING
BK	*Sandi the King Maker*.
	THE COMING OF SANDI
BK	*Sandi the King Maker*.
	THE RESOURCES OF CIVILIZATION
BK	*Sandi the King Maker*.
	THE HOUSE OF THE CHOSEN
BK	*Sandi the King Maker*.
	THE DEATH MARK
BK	*Sandi the King Maker*
Vol. 54	June to Nov. 1921 THE WOMAN IN THE HUT
BK	*Sandi the King maker*.
	THE KING FROM THE SOUTH
BK	*Sandi the King Maker*.
	THE PASSING OF MAJOR HAMILTON
BK	*Sandi the King Maker*.
	THE GREY BIRD THAT MOANED
BK	*Sandi the King Maker*.

	THE WAR IN THE TOFOLAKA
BK	*Sandi the King Maker.*
	WHAT HAPPENED TO HAMILTON
BK	*Sandi the King Maker.*
Vol. 55	Dec. 1921 to May 1922 A LESSON IN DIPLOMACY
BK	*Chick.* A Lesson in Diplomacy.
	A WRIT OF SUMMONS
BK	*Chick.* A Writ of Summons.
	CHICK
BK	*Chick.* Chick.
	CHICK. WAITER
BK	*Chick.* Chick. Waiter.
	FOR ONE NIGHT ONLY
BK	*Chick.* For one night only.
	THE FIRST DISPATCH
BK	*Chick.* The First Dispatch.
Vol. 56	June to Nov. 1922 COURAGE
BK	*Chick.* Courage.
	IN THE PUBLIC EYE
BK	*Chick.* In the Public Eye.
	THE BEATING OF THE MIDDLE-WEIGHT
BK	*Chick.* The Beating of the Middle-weight.
	THE MAN FROM TOULOUSE
BK	*Chick.* The Man from Toulouse.
	THE OILFIELD
BK	*Chick.* The Oilfield.
Vol. 59	Dec. 1923 to May 1924 THE CHRISTMAS PRINCESS (There were times when John Bennett . . .)
BK	*Circumstantial Evidence.* The Christmas Princess
BK	*Forty Eight Short Stories.* The Christmas Princess

244

Vol. 61	Dec. 1924 to May 1925 ON THE WITNEY ROAD. (Tom Curtis said nothing . . .)
BK	*The Governor of Chi-Foo*. On the Witney Road
BK	*Forty Eight Short Stories*. On the Witney Road.
Vol. 63	Dec. 1925 to May 1926 THE CHRISTMAS CUP (Colonel Desboro was an easy . . .)
BK	*Fighting Snub Reilly*. The Christmas Cup.
BK	*Forty Eight Short Stories*. The Christmas Cup.
BK	*The Undisclosed Client*. The Christmas Cup.
MG	*Royal Magazine*, 1929. He who could Ride.

Apr. 1932 EDGAR WALLACE: A REMINISCENCE —showing a reproduction of a charming letter E. W. sent to a 12 year old girl named Joan on 9 Apr. 1919 in answer to her request for him to write a Sanders or Bones story. His address given as:

71 Clarence Gate Gardens, N.W.1.

PAD 1764

Yes or No

| Vol. 26 | 10 Dec. 1910. 'UNCLE DICK' (Mr Agnew, |
| No. 352 | Magnate, gave the . . .) |

Magazines which contained work by Edgar Wallace and which are not listed in this bibliography.

Not only are they not represented in the files of the British Museum, but either the publishers themselves have ceased business, or else they do not hold file copies.

Hulton's Christmas Magazines.

Good Humour. (1937 and Educated Evans reprinted stories)

Jungle Tales (British edition) (Assumed Sanders or Bones Reprints)

Hush Magazine (1930) of which Edgar Wallace was editor.

The following magazine stories have been discovered just prior to going to press.

Argosy
April 1939. THE RISING OF THE ARKASAVA
June 1961. THE PROUD HORSE (Educated Evans left the Italian Club. . .)

Pictorial Magazine
27 Dec. 1924. Obvious part of a serial entitled 'Mystery Manor' probably the original story of 'Big Foot' as this character is mentioned a great deal.

Tit Bit Novels
No. 10, 16 Sept. 1911. THE PRICE A WOMAN PAYS (All that April had promised. . .) (complete original 25,000 word story believed only time of publication.)
No. 192 13 Mar. 1915 FIVE FATEFUL WORDS (Sir George Farringdon was arrested. . .) (competition story in which readers were invited to send five words from the novel which would cause the American detective to lose his case)
No. 209. 10 June. 1915 MEMOIRS OF THE SIGEE FAMILY (Mr Albert Sigee had a tale. . .)

With the permission of the Edgar Wallace estate the author, Francis Gerard, wrote three full-length novels featuring 'Sanders of the River' all published by Rich & Cowan.
THE RETURN OF SANDERS OF THE RIVER 1938
THE LAW OF THE RIVER 1939
THE JUSTICE OF SANDERS 1951
Francis Gerard died in Africa, the scene of the Sanders stories, a few years ago.

SPECIAL NOTE:
Only national newspaper stories have been recorded as it has been established that these tales were syndicated into hundreds of local newspapers, and indeed throughout the world.